Sugar,
I Love You

Sugar,
I Love You

Ravneet Gill

PAVILION

Conte

nts

Introduction	08
Cake	10
Biscuits	36
Cheesecake	52
Sweet Doughs	70
Fried Things	92
Tarts & Pies	110
Entremet	138
Ice Cream	172
Plated Desserts	184
Index	202
Thank You	206

Sugar
I Love

'You

When I eat something beautifully sweet, I feel like time stops.

I fantasize about sweet things. When I eat something beautifully sweet, I feel like time stops. An expert on weight-loss diets once said that all you need to say to yourself for success is: 'I've had enough chocolate cake for a lifetime, so the memories will keep me going.' But why live in a memory when you can have that piece of chocolate cake now? Especially when it might be the remarkably light, airy, intensely chocolatey cake of your dreams. Warmed for 20 seconds in the microwave with a tiny sprinkle of sea salt and served with cold pouring cream. You see, when I start thinking of my sweet memories, the sides of my cheeks start to water and all I want to do is satisfy that craving.

To me, airports are Loacker hazelnut wafers. They mean holiday and, when on holiday, I can plough through an XL pack in moments, without a care in the world. The smooth red packaging encasing its neatly packed – precise near Jenga-like – wafers satisfies something deep within me… and cements my association between comfort, Loacker wafers and being abroad on adventures.

My first book, *The Pastry Chef's Guide*, did its thing all right. It unexpectedly took off, with so many of you jumping on board with it, embracing that straight-to-the-point teacher vibe that I wanted. I felt like I couldn't dish out a full-colour recipe book such as this until I had broken down the fundamentals of pastry for you. The reality is that making sweet things isn't that hard and shouldn't be portrayed as such. As ever, and with everything, you should be in the now; lean into the sugar and have fun. It took me a while to realize that and, when I did, I baked better.

We say that we make mistakes, but mistakes – or even failures – shouldn't be feared in life or in baking. Instead, we should learn to view them as blessings. I ran one of the worst nights of my life a few years back, a speed-dating event for food lovers that went down the pan, along with my soul. Nevertheless, it taught me to value those experiences and to dive into failure across all aspects of my life. Failure and mistakes are how we learn and grow. Without them, we would constantly be floating along at average. So, after every mishap, look up at the sky and shout **THANK YOU** for your chance to learn. And do learn, because if you do, next time you will improve.

Now, I know what you're thinking: this is going to be about a bold, unashamed love of sugar… but it isn't. Or rather, it isn't *only* that. It's a celebration of the joy sweetness brings to our lives when it's married with other ingredients in perfect combinations. We all love to indulge in sweet things, but moderation is what makes me love sugar. Only when sugar is truly understood and used to balance pastry and desserts does it really shine. You'll find many recipes in this book that don't actually contain much sugar at all, and that's what makes it such a versatile and precious ingredient. Knowing when and how to use sugar is, in many ways, the essence of pastry and dessert-making.

So here we are, book number two, *Sugar, I Love You*. Because I really do. This book is all about just that: **LOVE**, displayed through absolutely brilliant recipes. I urge you to take the principles and base recipes in these pages and tweak and adjust them to fit your palate, always tasting as you go.

Cakes
Cakes
Cakes
Cakes

I find any excuse to eat cake, no special occasion is required.

Black forest gateau has to be one of my all-time favourite cakes: the light chocolate sponge, those canned cherries and fresh cream; chocolate ganache, too, if you're lucky. As a kid, I would beg my mum to buy me slices of it from our local cake shop. While the very definition of glamour back then was a traybake birthday cake from Tesco, a level up was Colin the Caterpillar, and at the top of the tree – a fresh cream cake from the bakery.

I remember baking really bad cakes as a teenager, creating a massive Jaffa Cake (what was that obsession with giant food? Or was it just me?), layer cakes for birthdays and cupcakes topped with the worst basic b*tch buttercream. I'm really sorry if you were one of those people who had to pretend to like any of these early attempts at baking. I truly thought I was in my element and even showed up to a job interview with a photo album of the cupcakes I had made. Yes, I really did that, a real photo album with real photos that I had to get printed off at Boots. I didn't get the job… for obvious reasons.

I didn't know back then that I would become a successful pastry chef, or that I'd eventually have the mental capacity to reflect and realize that I was really bad at it while growing up. I've just always adored sweet things. Cake means different things to different people. It can remind you of pivotal moments in your life, such as the cake you ate when you got dumped for the first time or *that* Victoria sponge from your sixteenth birthday. But I find any excuse to eat cake, no special occasion is required. I am happiest when eating it alone, on the sofa, with a fork, so please do remember to give me some cutlery – and some space – after you hand me a slice.

Now, unfortunately, in life you may meet others who don't reciprocate your love of cake. These people are not right for you. I once dated a man who didn't like sugar, which should have been the clearest sign that it wasn't going to work, but I ignored my gut instinct and went with it. Down the line, I was sitting at the table, eagerly anticipating an

after dinner slice of cake. I lifted it up with my hands, gazing at it with love, excited to put it in my mouth. Suddenly I felt a hand on my wrist, pulling the cake away. I turned my head to see the sugar-hater shaking his. He then mouthed, 'It will go straight to your hips.' Shock, horror and a big fat fingers up, I'm out.

And you know what? This isn't that unusual. My friend's former partner denied her a doughnut once after she'd already enjoyed an apple crumble (I knew it wouldn't work out from that moment). **READ THE SIGNS, HONEY.** Since making my mistake, I've learned. I now officially designate it compulsory that anyone who gets the luxury of dating me must love food, and – vitally – love that I love food (especially cake), too.

… I also learned never to take a photo album of the cupcakes you made as a teenager to a job interview. It doesn't make a good impression.

Mistake Cake

I want to start with this cake specifically. A cake that I was making in a rush, while trying to dance to Afrobeats and talking to a mate. While I was cleaning up, I noticed half my weighed flour still in a bowl on the worktop. I hadn't added it! Immediately I thought: damn, I'm going to have to make the whole thing again from scratch. However, when I took the cake out of the oven and ate a piece, I realized how my wrong was now right! The texture of this cake is so excellent that it has become my go-to layer sponge recipe when I want something moist, airy and light.

This layer cake requires no soaking syrup, so it's able to embrace the buttercream and jam in all their glory.

The whole egg buttercream will keep in the fridge for up to 3 days. It will harden up in there, so to use it you will need to put it into a stand mixer and beat it gently, either blowtorching the bowl to warm it slightly or gently melting a few tablespoons of the buttercream completely before returning it to the rest of the mixture in the mixer.

The buttercream holds very well once a cake has been coated. In fact, so well that the cake can then be frozen as a whole and defrosted when needed.

A NOTE: Double the quantity of buttercream if you want a thicker coating.

Mistake Cake

Makes a 20cm (8in) layer cake

For the sponge

375g unsalted butter, softened,
  plus extra for the tins
10g/2 tsp vanilla extract
270g caster sugar
100g light brown sugar
6 eggs, lightly beaten
225g self-raising flour
2g/2 large pinches of fine salt
finely grated zest of 2 unwaxed
  lemons

For the whole egg buttercream

50ml water
200g caster sugar
2 eggs (total weight 100g)
280g unsalted butter, softened
  and cubed
pinch of fine salt
finely grated citrus zest, vanilla
  extract or other flavourings of
  your choice (optional)

For the filling

300g of your chosen jam to layer

Preheat the oven to 160°C fan/180°C/gas mark 4. Butter the sides of four 20cm (8in) sandwich cake tins and line the bases with baking paper.

Beat the butter with the vanilla for 5 minutes, until super-smooth. With the paddle attachment add both the sugars and beat for 10 minutes at a medium speed, then scrape the bowl down and beat for a further 5 minutes. Add the eggs in three stages, beating well after each addition.

In a separate bowl, stir together the flour, salt and lemon zest, then add this to the batter. Gently mix until fully combined.

Weigh the total amount of batter, then distribute one-quarter of it into each prepared tin, smoothing over the top with a palette knife.

Bake for 18 minutes, until a skewer inserted comes out clean. Allow to cool before removing from the tins. (At this stage the cakes can now be stacked with a sheet of baking paper between them, tightly wrapped and frozen for up to 1 month. Simply defrost fully before filling and icing.)

For the buttercream, place the measured water and sugar into a saucepan over a medium heat. We are taking the sugar to 121°C, so keep a thermometer in it.

Start gently whipping the eggs in a stand mixer until pale and frothy.

When the sugar reaches 119°C, remove it from the heat (the residual heat from the pan will help it climb to 121°C by the time it gets to the mixer).

With the mixer on a medium speed, gently pour the hot sugar syrup in a thin stream down the side of the bowl, being careful not to let it touch the whisk. Whisk until cool; the bowl should no longer feel hot to touch.

Start adding the butter, a chunk at a time, while the machine is still going. Once all the butter has been added, throw in the salt and any optional flavourings and whisk until combined.

Switch the whisk attachment for the paddle attachment and mix for a further few minutes. The paddle will help to knock out any air bubbles, which will mean a smooth finish on the cake.

Spread a layer of buttercream and jam over three of the cakes, then sandwich them together with the final cake on top. Coat the top and sides with the remaining buttercream.

Ras Malai Cake

When I worked in an Indian restaurant (as a chef rather than a pastry chef), everyone there thought I was mad. I mean, that's a given, but their specific complaint was that I would request that the pastry chefs save the ras malai milk for me so I could drink pints of it during service. For those who don't know what ras malai is, let me enlighten you. It's an Indian pudding made of light milk dumplings, soaked in sweet, gently spiced milk. The milk contains notes of cardamom, crushed pistachios and sometimes flaked almonds; saffron if you're lucky, too.

A while back, my friend Mattie bought me a cupcake that was soaked in the stuff and it was sensational, so I thought we should make a whole cake based on it. This cake is baked in a disposable foil container, so it soaks up all that milk. You should take it with you to a barbecue or a picnic, give everyone a spoon and just get stuck in. I guarantee your friends will ask you to make it again and again.

Makes a 31 x 25cm (12 x 9in) foil container of cake

For the cake

4 eggs, lightly beaten
175g caster sugar
1 tsp baking powder
pinch of fine salt
200g plain flour
20ml neutral oil
280ml whole milk
200ml double cream
140g condensed milk
3 cardamom pods, lightly crushed
small pinch of saffron threads
1 tbsp ground pistachios
10 roasted almonds, crushed

To serve

300ml gently whipped cream
handful of crushed pistachios
handful of roasted flaked almonds

Preheat the oven to 160°C fan/180°C/gas mark 4.

Using a stand mixer or electric whisk, whisk the eggs gently on a medium speed with the sugar until thick and luscious. The mixture should be at ribbon stage (thick enough to hold its shape when drizzled back on top of itself).

In a separate bowl, stir together the baking powder, salt and plain flour.

In three batches, sift the flour mixture over the egg mixture and fold it in gently. Drizzle the oil in gradually and fold in as you pour, making sure not to over-mix.

Pour the mixture into a 31 x 25cm (12 x 9in) foil container and bake for 30 minutes, or until a skewer inserted comes out clean.

Meanwhile, in a saucepan gently warm the milk, cream and condensed milk with the cardamom, saffron, ground pistachios and crushed almonds until steaming. Take off the heat.

When the cake is baked, remove it from the oven and allow to cool for 15 minutes.

Poke holes with a cocktail stick all over the cake and pour over the slightly warm (but not hot) milk mixture evenly (make sure you remove the cardamom pods).

Leave at room temperature until cool, then place in the fridge, ideally overnight, so the flavours all get used to each other and have time to properly chill out. It will keep in there for up to 3 days.

To finish, top the cake with gently whipped cream, crushed pistachios and flaked almonds. For extra luxury, add saffron to a basic sugar syrup (see page 100) and drizzle generously over the top, before serving chilled.

Crème Fraîche Loaf, Roasted Plums and Pistachio Cream

Rosy Rong spent ages developing a yogurt sponge for the legendary St. JOHN restaurant in London, and it was a really lovely addition to the summer menu, when seasonal fruit was in abundance. This holds up beautifully and also freezes very well. Serve it by the slice, gently toasted and buttered, with the best seasonal fruit you can find – we used apricots and fresh raspberries here, but I urge you to try the plums and pistachio cream version!

Makes a 900g loaf

For the loaf

6 eggs, lightly beaten
320g caster sugar
180g crème fraîche
finely grated zest and juice of 1 large orange (you need 40ml of juice)
70g unsalted butter, melted
330g plain flour
4g/scant 1 tsp baking powder
1g/large pinch of fine salt

For the plums and pistachio cream

4 plums
30g caster sugar
200g double cream
2 tbsp pistachio praline paste
1 tbsp honey
pinch of sea salt flakes

Preheat the oven to 160°C fan/180°C/gas mark 4. Line a 900g loaf tin with baking paper on the base and sides.

Gently whisk together the eggs and sugar – by hand is totally fine here as we are not trying to create volume, we are just combining them.

In a separate bowl, whisk together the crème fraîche, orange zest and juice and melted butter. Add this to the whisked eggs and stir to combine.

In another bowl, stir together the flour, baking powder and salt, then add to the batter. Use a whisk to make sure it's all fully mixed together.

Pour into the prepared loaf tin and bake for 50 minutes. Turn the cake around in the oven, then bake for a further 25 minutes, or until a skewer inserted comes out clean. Remove from the oven and leave to cool in the tin.

For the plums, cut in half, remove the stones and place in a roasting tin. Sprinkle the sugar on top and roast for 10–15 minutes until the fruit has softened and the skin has blistered. Leave to cool.

To make the pistachio cream, whip the double cream to soft peaks, then add the pistachio praline paste, honey and salt and whisk gently until it all comes together.

Toast slices of the crème fraîche loaf on a hot griddle and serve buttered, with roasted plums and pistachio cream on the side. Joyous.

LPC (Lazy Person's Cake)

For your eating pleasure, I spent weeks testing different variations of chocolate cake. I knew what I wanted: something wonderfully moist, a touch bitter, light, quick-to-make and beautiful. The perfect lazy person's cake. It had to be a gleaming beauty that looked like you'd spent forever on it, when in reality it involved very little effort. We make this cake for people we care about, but don't have much time for. Fringe friends, you might say. I had made 40–50 different versions of this cake by the time I spoke to my friend Terri Mercieca about it. And what's better than two pastry brains? Five pastry brains! So we decided to get together with Edd Kimber, Jon Hogan and Lily Vanilli to conduct a few chocolate cake tests. We changed the acidity of batters by using homemade kefir, soured cream and buttermilk, and adjusted the fat content by experimenting with vegetable oil, melted butter and olive oil. We changed the type of cocoa powder, varied the amounts of raising agent, altered the type of flour and even tested packet cake mixes.

And to make it even better, everyone made their own favourite chocolate cake to start with. Edd made a beautiful two-layered rich, glossy cake. Terri went rogue and impressed us all with a vegan version. Lily joined us virtually over WhatsApp, teasing us with photos of her lovely cake, while Jon blew us all away by making his own chocolate from scratch!

By the end of it, I think we were all pretty sick of chocolate cake (we proved that it *is* possible), but we all had our favourite iteration, too. Mine involves buttermilk and olive oil. When I told Terri the concept of the lazy person's cake she said: 'Dude, LPC, that's what you gotta call it' – and here it is!

LPC (Lazy Person's Cake)

Makes a 20cm (8in) cake

For the wet cake mix

175ml olive oil, not overly strong, plus extra for the tins

2 eggs

175ml buttermilk

170ml boiling water

5g/1 tsp instant coffee

For the dry cake mix

125g caster sugar

125g light brown sugar

80g cocoa powder

230g plain flour

5g/1 tsp sea salt flakes

10g/2 tsp bicarbonate of soda

5g/1 tsp baking powder

For the malt chocolate ganache

150g 70 per cent cocoa solids chocolate, chopped

50g 55 per cent cocoa solids chocolate, chopped

pinch of sea salt flakes

300g double cream

1 tbsp malt extract (alternatively use black treacle, maple syrup or honey)

I want to blaze through this recipe as quick as you, so here we go! Preheat the oven to 160°C fan/180°C/gas mark 4. Grease two 20cm (8in) cake tins with oil, then line with baking paper.

Weigh all the dry cake mix ingredients into a large bowl and stir together with a whisk to fully combine. (If the sugar is lumpy, you will have to sift it.)

Weigh all the wet cake mix ingredients, except the water and coffee, into a large bowl and whisk together. Make the coffee in a cup with the measured boiling water and instant coffee, pour it into the wet ingredients bowl and stir well.

Add the dry mix to the wet mix and stir well with a whisk to combine.

Divide the mixture evenly between the prepared tins (if you want to be precise, you can weigh the total batter, then divide it exactly in half).

Bake for 35 minutes, or until a skewer inserted comes out clean.

Remove from the oven and allow to cool in the tin for 20 minutes before flipping onto a wire rack (allow to cool fully before adding the ganache you're about to make).

To make the ganache, put both the chocolates and the salt in a large heatproof bowl.

In a saucepan, heat the cream with the malt extract until steaming but not boiling.

Pour the hot cream over the chocolate and leave for 1 minute. Use a whisk to stir the ganache from the middle outwards – so as not to whisk in any air – until silky and beautiful. Let the ganache sit for 10 minutes.

Take a large plate with a lip. Place a cooled cake on the plate and spoon over enough ganache to cover the top. Don't worry if it spills over the edges, we kind of want this. Place the next cake on top. Pour the remaining ganache all over the top, without a care in the world. Use a spoon to guide it over, making sure plenty of ganache is falling down the sides. Put the cake in the fridge for 20–30 minutes.

Remove the cake from the fridge and, using a small offset palette knife, scoop up the set ganache from the edges of the plate and spread over the sides to create a smooth finish. It really is *that* easy and effortless. You'll have your friends thinking you really care…

This cake keeps best in an airtight container at room temperature for 3 days. If storing in the fridge, allow to come to room temp before eating – it'll be much nicer! I recommend warming up a slice in the microwave for 20 seconds and pouring cold cream all over it.

Toffee Apple Self-Saucing Pudding

Proper old school, self-saucing puddings have been around for yonks and I don't know why more people don't make them more often. They are very effective and really good when you're short of time and want to cook something impressive for a dinner with friends. It's more of a comforting winter dessert than a summer one, though.

The way this works is by making a light cake batter with enough raising agent in it; here we benefit from a chemical reaction via the baking powder that is already in the self-raising flour. The liquid poured on top is heavier than the light batter, so it sinks to the bottom while the cake rises, mingling together to create a rich sauce. So when you delve into the pudding you are treated to a wonderfully light sponge that comes with its own sauce, and you didn't really have to do much.

A NOTE: This pudding is on the edge between sweet and tart; if you prefer a sweeter pudding, up the brown sugar that is scattered over the top by 20g.

Serves 6

150g unsalted butter, softened
120g caster sugar
2–3 Bramley apples, peeled, cored and roughly chopped into 2.5cm (1in) chunks (roughly 250g chunks)
2 eggs, lightly beaten
150g self-raising flour
pinch of fine salt
¼ tsp ground cinnamon
2 tbsp whole milk
400ml cloudy apple juice
25g cornflour
60g dark brown sugar

Preheat the oven to 160°C fan/ 180°C/gas mark 4.

Start by creaming the butter and sugar together in a stand mixer, or by hand until pale and fluffy.

Place the chopped apples in a 20cm (8in) ovenproof dish or closed bottom tin (this is important so that the liquid doesn't leak out), there should be enough to cover the base.

Add the eggs to the butter mixture and beat in, then add the flour, salt and cinnamon. Pour in the milk and stir together to form a batter, then spoon the batter over the apples.

Warm the apple juice gently in a saucepan and put the cornflour into a medium heatproof bowl. When the apple juice is warm, pour it over the cornflour and stir continuously until thoroughly mixed.

Scatter the dark brown sugar over the top of the batter in the dish. Evenly pour over the warmed apple juice mix, then place the dish on a baking tray.

Bake for 35 minutes, or until a skewer inserted into the cake part comes out clean. (If the skewer goes all the way to the bottom it will touch the sauce.)

Take out of the oven and serve warm with double cream, custard, ice cream or – in true Quo Vadis chef and pudding lover, Jeremy Lee style – all three.

Brown Butter and Chocolate Chip Financiers

These little cakes are magical. When I gave some, warm, to my next-door neighbour Jay, he texted me immediately, saying they made him dance with joy while he ate them. Brown buttery, chocolatey, salty, sweet, lovely, lovely stuff – and a brilliant way to use up any leftover egg whites.

Makes 12

120g butter, plus extra (optional) for the moulds
50ml boiling water
5g/1 tsp instant coffee
150g icing sugar
70g ground almonds
75g plain flour
2.5g/½ tsp baking powder
pinch of sea salt flakes, crushed
200g egg whites
80g mini chocolate chips
flaked almonds, to top

Melt the butter in a saucepan and keep heating until it is browned and smells nutty. Let the brown butter cool until it's no longer hot to touch. Weigh the brown butter again, you should be left with 100g.

Make the coffee with the measured boiling water and instant coffee, then allow it to cool down so it's warm, not hot.

Sift all the dry ingredients into a bowl and stir to combine evenly. Add the coffee, egg whites and brown butter. Stir evenly and gently with a spatula until the mix is homogeneous. Scrape down the sides of the bowl and place the bowl of batter in the fridge for 1 hour.

Preheat the oven to 160°C fan/180°C/gas mark 4.

Remove from the fridge and stir through the chocolate chips, weigh 60g of batter each into 12 round silicone moulds, or buttered muffin tray holes, then sprinkle some flaked almonds on top.

Bake for 23 minutes, then remove from the oven and remove the cakes from the moulds.

Eat these warm, cold or simply reheat in a microwave, enjoying with a splash of cold cream.

Cherry and Ricotta Cake

This sponge is **SO GOOD**, I don't think I know anyone who has failed making it. You can switch out the cherries for another seasonal fruit (taste it first and be the judge here!). Alternatively, a friend of mine bakes the sponge without the fruit and uses it as a layer cake.

Makes a 20cm (8in) cake

140g unsalted butter

220g caster sugar

finely grated zest of 1 unwaxed lemon or orange

3 eggs

pinch of fine salt

165g plain flour, plus ½ tbsp for dredging the cherries

2½ tsp baking powder

250g ricotta

10ml/2 tsp amaretto (optional)

300g pitted cherries

handful of demerara sugar

juice of ½ orange, warmed (optional)

Preheat the oven to 160°C fan/180°C/gas mark 4 and line a 20cm (8in) cake tin with baking paper.

Beat the butter and sugar together with the zest until pale and fluffy. Scrape down the bowl and add the eggs one at a time, beating well between additions.

Stir together the salt, flour and baking powder in a separate bowl and then add to the batter. Scrape down the bowl once more and make sure it is evenly mixed.

Add the ricotta and gently mix, then finally stir through the amaretto if using. Scrape into the prepared tin. Toss the cherries in the ½ tbsp flour, then sprinkle them evenly over the cake batter.

Bake for 1 hour 10 minutes. After 45 minutes, sprinkle over the handful of demerara sugar to give it a nice crunch on top. At the end of cooking time, check the cake is baked by inserting a skewer and making sure it comes out clean. Leave to cool in the tin.

When the cake has cooled, brush over the warmed orange juice to give it a slight shine on top, if you like.

This cake keeps for 3 days at room temperature in a sealed container.

Passion Cake

My mum had been banging on about this for a while, it's a cake that she reminisces about eating over and over again during her glamour days. The days when she stumbled into a job in Park Lane and would go to Richoux tea rooms on her break. She describes it as 'passion fruit cake', and I spent ages trying to figure out a recipe for the one she was describing. I think my mum has fantasized about this cake so much that she doesn't really remember it herself. After a lot of back and forth, it turns out that the cake is called 'passion cake' and doesn't contain any passion fruit whatsoever. My mum loves passion fruit a lot though, so I thought: why not put it in the icing? It will keep her quiet for a bit. The icing is easy to put together when in a rush, smooth and tasty. Just be careful to not over-beat the cream cheese, or it will turn into unsalvageable slop.

A NOTE: My mum loves icing and would prefer that I doubled the amount here so that it covers the sides of the cake. I disagree and like that thing called 'balance', so I stick with a single batch, as pictured. However, it's not about being right, it's about being kind, so if you prefer more, double the quantities and go for it.

Passion Cake

Makes a 20cm (8in) cake

For the cake

50g walnuts

2 eggs, lightly beaten

260g light brown sugar

½ tsp fine salt

1 tsp ground cinnamon

½ tsp ground ginger

½ tsp bicarbonate of soda

1 tsp baking powder

150g plain flour

100g wholemeal flour

260ml neutral oil

1 ripe banana

190g grated carrot

a few drops of orange
   blossom water

For the icing

75g unsalted butter, softened

45g caster sugar

pinch of sea salt flakes

320g cream cheese, at room
   temperature

1 passion fruit

2 tbsp icing sugar

Preheat the oven to 160°C fan/180°C/gas mark 4. Line two 20cm (8in) cake tins with baking paper.

Spread the walnuts over a baking tray. Toast in the oven for 12–15 minutes, stirring halfway through. Cool completely, then crush the nuts. Set aside.

Whisk the eggs with the sugar in a stand mixer on a medium speed until pale, thick and fluffy.

In a separate bowl, mix together the salt, ground spices, both raising agents and both flours.

Pour the oil into the egg mixture slowly, feeding it in bit by bit, and making sure it is fully incorporated before the next addition. Separately mush up the banana properly with a fork and add this to the egg mixture.

Add the dry ingredients and mix well until fully incorporated. Stir in the carrot, toasted crushed walnuts and orange blossom water. Divide the mixture between the prepared tins.

Bake for 30–35 minutes, or until a skewer inserted comes out clean. Leave to cool in the tins.

For the icing, beat the butter and caster sugar together for a few minutes until fluffy. Scrape down the sides of the bowl, then add the salt and all the cream cheese. Beat this for a few minutes until it *just* comes together. Do not over-mix it!

Scrape out the seeds and juice from the passion fruit and tip into the mixer. Sift in the icing sugar and beat again quickly until combined.

Use immediately, or store in the fridge until you are ready to spread it in between and on top of the cooled cakes.

This cake will keep in an airtight container in the fridge for 3 days.

Olive Oil, Semolina, Cardamom and Rose Cake

Some people don't like the flavour of rose, and I do get it. Too much rose on a single occasion can put you off for life; used incorrectly, it can feel as though you're swallowing a mouthful of perfume. But I'm a professional, babes, I've used it mindfully and intentionally here to really lift this cake. Balanced in spice, the aroma in the kitchen once you've made this is nothing short of beautiful. The olive oil contributes to a moist crumb and a cake that keeps for days without drying out. This needs no icing or topping; adding those would simply take away from the delicate spicing.

Makes a 20cm (8in) cake

For the cake

3 green cardamom pods
2 eggs, lightly beaten
130g caster sugar
100ml olive oil
finely grated zest and juice
  of 1 unwaxed lemon
100g Greek yogurt
4 drops of rose extract
70g plain flour
40g fine semolina
1½ tsp baking powder
pinch of fine salt

For the syrup

50g caster sugar
60ml/4 tbsp water
2 drops of rose extract, or juice
  of ½ lemon

Preheat the oven to 160°C fan/180°C/gas mark 4. Line a 20cm (8in) cake tin with baking paper.

Using a spice grinder, blitz the cardamom pods whole until super-fine. Alternatively crush well in a pestle and mortar.

Whisk the eggs and sugar together until pale, thick and fluffy. Drizzle in the olive oil gradually, whisking gently until fully mixed; it should emulsify like a mayonnaise.

Squeeze the lemon juice into the yogurt and then stir this into the egg mixture, adding the lemon zest, rose extract and blitzed cardamom.

In a separate bowl, stir together the dry ingredients with a whisk. Add the dry ingredients to the batter and stir until fully combined. Pour into the prepared tin and bake for 30 minutes.

Meanwhile, prepare the syrup by heating the sugar and measured water together in a saucepan until the sugar has dissolved. Add the rose extract or lemon juice.

Remove the cake from the oven and allow to cool in the tin for 10 minutes. Poke holes in the cake all over using a toothpick, then evenly drizzle over the syrup.

Allow the cake to fully cool in the tin before removing and eating in bliss. This will keep for 3–4 days, covered, at room temperature.

Bis

Bis

Bis

Bis

cuits

cuits

cuits

cuits

Who on earth would share a single biscuit?

It's a serious question, and the first words uttered by my friends during our afternoon biscuit chat. You see, I think biscuits are incredibly personal; everyone has their own relationship with them. You can tell a lot about people by their choice of biscuit. Here is what I can tell about some of my friends…

Sarah and I have spent many evenings eating biscuits together in my bedroom. Normally I would perish the thought of crumbs in my room, but, during that period in my life, it was the cleanest safe space I had.

I adore Sarah because she loves biscuits. Okay, that's not quite true, but I think our shared love brought us closer together; she has a mad appetite for someone so petite. And we are both really loud and shouty together, the perfect duo on a night out. Sarah's got this weird habit, though, she loves big cookies but they have to be **JUST** right. Not too soft, but also not crunchy. You know how she goes about finding the right ones? By squeezing them in the packet in the shop. Yeah, that's Sarah.

Sarah's favourites include not-too-soft, not-too-crunchy fat cookies, chocolate chip Marylands, Jaffa cakes and custard creams.

Natalie is something else. In Natalie's biscuit tin when she was growing up you would find a mix of biscuits: ginger nuts **AND** Ritz crackers. Natalie is the type of person who buys a whole Christmas cake just to eat the icing. The type of friend who will consistently choose the citrus dessert and stick up for you no matter what, while simultaneously schooling you about yourself.

During a chat over tea, Natalie eats custard creams and Fox's Golden Crunch Creams (but only for the filling). We get into tackling how to deal with a date who comes over and then won't leave.

Nat says the way to get a guy to leave is to walk him to the train station. She wants him to tell her where they're going and what he will be cooking for her on the second date. Someone like Nat can't be as high-powered as she is without clarity and rules.

Harriet – who loves DIY, making her own biscuits (her favourites are 50% more chocolate than biscuit), gin and bath salts – says that going for a coffee is the only first date you should consider. By the time you've drunk a coffee, you will have decided if you don't like someone… **NEXT!**

There's so many people in Chell's house that biscuits don't last for long. Chell doesn't really have a sweet tooth. It does disappoint me, but Chell makes up for it by being a very kind soul, and a Capricorn. If you don't like sweet things, you've at least got to be kind. If you've got neither of those qualities, we can't really hang out.

Bhavin has a few biscuit tins on the go, he's my kind of guy. Bhavin enjoys the simple pleasures of a nice biscuit and a really good cup of coffee. Despite having quite an important job, you'll often find him skiving in the local coffee shop, napping in the cafeteria or using his laptop as an umbrella (true story). Bhavin says that when growing up, when his neighbour would give his family a tin of Fox's biscuits for Christmas, he knew he couldn't open the tin because his mum would re-gift it. Now he has cut loose and opens biscuit tins with abandon.

Alvin, a social media manager, is a rare diamond in the group as we are rarely graced with his presence; he would rather eat a tin of Ferrero Rocher while rolling his eyes at Bhavin. Oh, and someone better film him while he's at it.

When I was growing up, biscuits were in abundance, along with the contents of the snack drawer. Spending my first few years living above a corner shop that my dad owned assisted in the ease of this. Throughout my life, the biscuit tin has always been full, first in my mother's home and now in mine. My mum has always maintained that you've got to be ready in case anyone pops over. Biji – my grandma – moved in with my family a few years ago and I think it's been a blessing. As mad and quirky as she is, getting to spend time with her is invaluable. Biji has always been a biscuit icon in my eyes, she's got her priorities right. Two biscuit tins in her wardrobe with two different types on the go, usually malted milk and rich tea. In the kitchen there's two more, this time shortbread and custard creams. The only way she would choose a chocolate biscuit (which are some of my favourites) is if I told her I got them for free; then she'll make a point of eating them.

I always go for a custard cream. Or a bourbon. Or a cookie. Or anything with chocolate. Luckily for me, I was brought up to have a few different types on the go, so I'm not bound by any one variety at a time.

GRATEFUL.

Rav In Maryland

One of the most sought-after cookies in my childhood biscuit tin was the iconic Maryland cookie, with its short texture and mini chocolate chips. It definitely treads a fine line between being a bit too hard and being weirdly addictive.

I tested quite a few versions of this recipe and came to find that oil, a bit of butter and golden syrup gave these cookies just the texture and taste I was looking for. These are stupidly addictive.

I can't wait for you to make a batch and see what I mean.

This recipe can be made vegan by replacing the butter with vegetable fat (just be sure to use vegan chocolate, too).

Makes 30 small cookies

60ml neutral oil
20g/1 tbsp golden syrup
130g plain flour
½ tsp baking powder
¼ tsp bicarbonate of soda
small pinch of sea salt flakes
75g light brown sugar
30g unsalted butter, softened
50g dark chocolate, chopped
　　into small pieces

Whisk the oil and golden syrup together in a small bowl.

In a separate bowl, stir together the flour, baking powder, bicarbonate of soda and salt. Add the sugar and mix well to combine, then add the butter and mix really well until the butter disappears into the flour. Pour in the oil and syrup mixture and mix until a dough forms, then finally add the chopped chocolate and mix again.

Scoop the mixture onto a work surface and roll into a cylinder shape, roughly 23 x 5cm (9 x 2in). Wrap the cylinder tightly in clingfilm or baking paper and place on a tray. Refrigerate for 4 hours and then freeze for 2 hours so the dough is solid when you chop it (it really helps).

When you're ready to bake, preheat the oven to 160°C fan/180°C/ gas mark 4. Line two large baking trays with baking paper.

Using a sharp knife, slice the biscuit dough into 5mm (¼in) slices and place on the prepared trays, leaving plenty of space between each.

Bake for 15 minutes until golden, then allow to cool on the trays before eating. These cookies will stay crunchy and keep really well in an airtight container at room temperature.

Not-What-You-Think Chocolate Cookies

I think these are best eaten while wearing red nail polish and plentiful gold rings. That way, you get the full dramatic effect when you break one open, as this dark chocolate cookie dough is wrapped around a piece of white chocolate.

A NOTE: Cheap, own-brand white chocolate works best here.

Makes 7

50g dark chocolate, chopped
100g dark brown soft sugar
25g caster sugar
60g unsalted butter, softened
1 egg, lightly beaten
110g plain flour
10g/2 tsp cornflour
15g/1 tbsp cocoa powder
½ tsp bicarbonate of soda
105g white chocolate, in a bar
sea salt flakes

Put the dark chocolate into a heatproof bowl over a saucepan of simmering water, making sure the bowl does not touch the water. Leave to melt, then allow to cool to room temperature.

Cream together both sugars with the butter until pale and fluffy. Scrape down the bowl, add the egg and beat together. Pour in the cooled melted chocolate and mix.

In a separate bowl, stir together the flour, cornflour, cocoa powder and bicarbonate of soda until evenly combined. Tip into the batter and mix until there are no lumps, then scrape into a container and place in the fridge until set; this should take 2–4 hours.

Divide the dough into seven 50–55g balls and flatten each slightly.

Chop the white chocolate into 15g portions; it's fine if this amount is in more than 1 chunk, just bunch the bits together.

Place one 15g portion of white chocolate in the middle of each round of cookie dough, then fold up the sides to enclose the chocolate completely. Put these on a baking tray lined with baking paper and refrigerate overnight (or freeze straight away).

Preheat the oven to 170°C fan/190°C/gas mark 5. Make sure that the cookie dough balls have enough space between them to spread out, then bake for 14 minutes (or 15–16 minutes from frozen).

Allow the cookies to cool on the tray. Top with a tiny sprinkle of sea salt flakes before eating.

Oaty Terri Biscuits

My friend Terri means a lot to me. She is one of the most talented pastry chefs I know and I respect her hugely. We met because I kept pestering her for a job, but it just so happened that I never managed to land one with her, as our timings were always off: I would start a new role just as Terri needed someone, and vice versa!

Despite this, we formed a solid friendship based on the firm foundation of both of us loving sugar. Terri runs a successful ice cream sandwich business and is a wonderful person to bounce ideas off. During recipe testing for this book, I often asked Terri for her honest opinion. One of her most common notes to me was always: more salt! And I love this. As a pastry chef, you need to know your boundaries with salt, and Terri definitely knows hers.

I wanted to make an oaty malt biscuit in homage to Terri, as she is well-known for an oaty-malty ice cream sandwich that is the stuff of dreams. Terri, please add more salt to suit your palate!

PS I'm glad the universe didn't allow us to work together, as I'm sure we are better friends for it!

PPS You'll need ten 7cm (2¾in) metal rings for these.

Makes 10

For the biscuits

50g unsalted butter, plus extra for the rings
70g golden syrup
½ tsp bicarbonate of soda
65g jumbo oats
40g flaked almonds
25g plain flour
10g/2 tsp malt powder
¼ tsp sea salt flakes

For the coating

10g/2 tsp coconut oil
40g dark chocolate, chopped

Preheat the oven to 180°C fan/200°C/gas mark 6.

In a saucepan, heat the butter and syrup together until bubbling. Add the bicarbonate of soda and whisk until frothy. Take off the heat.

In a separate bowl, stir together the remaining ingredients, then stir them into the hot syrup mixture until evenly coated.

Line a large baking tray with baking paper. Liberally butter ten 7cm (2¾in) metal rings and place on the prepared tray. Spoon 1 large tbsp of mixture into each ring and press to make it an even layer.

Bake for 10 minutes, then remove the tray from the oven and, while still hot, lift off the metal rings. Leave to cool.

For the coating, melt the coconut oil in a small saucepan. Pour over the chopped chocolate in a heatproof bowl and stir until melted.

Dip the bases of the biscuits into the chocolate and place on a tray lined with baking paper. Place in the fridge for 10 minutes until the chocolate has set.

Gingernuts with White Chocolate Cream

Gingernuts are that crunchy British staple that appear every so often in the biscuit tin. I love the warmth that you get from the ground ginger, while the silkiness of the cream filling here adds a great contrast to the snap of the biscuit. Both my friends Natalie and Harriet love Fox's Ginger Crunch Creams, so this is a little nod to them.

Makes 30 gingernuts, or 15 filled biscuits

For the gingernuts

100g unsalted butter
100g light brown sugar
30g golden syrup
½ tsp ground ginger
pinch of fine salt
¼ tsp bicarbonate of soda
170g self-raising flour
2 tbsp whole milk

For the filling

30g white chocolate, chopped
70g unsalted butter, softened
50g cream cheese, at room
  temperature
pinch of fine salt

Beat the butter, sugar and syrup together until pale and thick. In a separate bowl, stir together the ground ginger, salt, bicarbonate of soda and flour, then add this to the butter mixture and beat until combined. Trickle in the milk and stir to evenly mix.

Scoop the mixture out onto a large sheet of baking paper and roll into a 30cm (12in) cylinder. Wrap in clingfilm and refrigerate for 30 minutes to firm up.

Preheat the oven to 160°C fan/180°C/gas mark 4.

Slice the cylinder of dough into 5mm (¼in) slices. Place on two large baking trays lined with baking paper, spacing the cookies well apart.

Bake for 15–18 minutes, or until golden. Allow to cool on the tray.

For the filling, melt the white chocolate in a large heatproof bowl over a pan of simmering water then leave to cool to room temperature for 30 minutes.

Beat the butter and cream cheese together until homogeneous, then fold in the cooled melted chocolate and the salt.

Place the filling in the fridge to chill, then pipe or spread it on the flat side of half the biscuits and top with the other halves. Store in an airtight container at room temperature.

Orange, Pecan and Milk Chocolate Cookies

You can, of course, eat cookies at any time of the year, however these in particular work very well around Christmas time, as they smell and taste very festive. The pre-bake dip in demerara sugar gives them a really satisfying crunch.

The cookie dough balls freeze really well, and will keep in an airtight container in the freezer for up to 1 month. Simply bake them from frozen, adding an extra 1–2 minutes to the baking time.

Makes 12

110g unsalted butter, softened
25g dark brown sugar
100g caster sugar
25g golden syrup
finely grated zest of 2 large
    oranges
1 egg, lightly beaten
190g plain flour
¼ tsp bicarbonate of soda
½ tsp baking powder
pinch of salt
120g milk chocolate, chopped
85g pecan nuts, roasted
demerara sugar, for dipping

Beat together the butter, both sugars and the syrup until pale and fluffy. Add the orange zest, scrape the bowl down and continue to beat until mixed. Add the egg and stir in.

In a separate bowl, mix together all the dry ingredients. Stir these into the butter mixture, then mix in the chocolate and pecans.

Place in a container and chill for 2–4 hours. Shape into 60g balls and chill in the fridge overnight. At this point, you can also freeze them, if you like (see recipe introduction).

When ready to bake, preheat the oven to 170°C fan/190°C/gas mark 5 and line a large baking tray with baking paper.

Dip each ball of dough into a bowl of demerara sugar and then space them well apart on the prepared baking tray.

Bake for 12–14 minutes, then leave to cool on the tray.

Roasted Hazelnut, Blueberry and Mascarpone Cookies

These are a softer-style cookie, my nan loves them when she can't be bothered to put her teeth in. She will pick out the blueberries though, as she can't stand dried fruit; something we will always disagree on.

Makes about 25

90g dried blueberries
100g unsalted butter, softened
100g mascarpone
2 egg yolks
140g caster sugar
150g roasted hazelnuts, 50g of these ground, 100g of these lightly chopped
½ tsp baking powder
pinch of fine salt
200g plain flour

Boil the kettle, put the dried blueberries in a bowl and pour over enough boiling water to cover. Set aside while you make the dough.

In a large bowl, beat the butter and mascarpone together, then stir in the egg yolks, then the sugar.

In a separate bowl, stir together the ground hazelnuts, baking powder, salt and flour, then add to the mascarpone bowl. Mix until a loose dough forms.

Strain off the water from the blueberries and pat them with kitchen paper to remove excess moisture.

Stir the blueberries and chopped hazelnuts into the mix, then rest the batter in the fridge for 30 minutes to firm up.

Shape into 30g balls.

Preheat the oven to 160°C fan/180°C/gas mark 4 and line two large baking trays with baking paper.

Space the cookie dough balls out on the two prepared trays, spacing them well apart, then bake for 18 minutes. Allow to cool on the tray.

Indian Semolina Shortbread (Nankhatai)

These are classic Indian biscuits traditionally eaten with tea. One of my mum's best friends, Tara Gahir, makes the absolute best versions, so buttery and melt-in-the-mouth that, when she brings a box over, none of us can stop eating them. Everything Tara makes is addictive and delicious; she really does have a magic way with food… snacks in particular.

These biscuits are eggless; the combination of butter (or traditionally ghee) and fine semolina gives them their distinct character and taste.

Makes about 17

175g unsalted butter, softened
85g icing sugar
85g fine semolina
55g chickpea flour
110g self-raising flour
pinch of salt

Preheat the oven to 120°C fan/140°C/gas mark 1. Line a baking tray with baking paper.

Cream the butter and sugar together until light and fluffy.

Mix the rest of the ingredients in to make a smooth dough, then rest in the fridge for 10 minutes.

Divide the dough into small balls (about 30g each if you're measuring) and cut a cross on top of each.

Space out on the prepared tray and bake for 20 minutes.

Allow to cool on the tray before eating.

Dutch Shortcake Biscuits Dipped in Chocolate

Unlike traditional firm biscuit dough, these are made using a soft dough that's piped into swirls or batons before being baked. The key to getting a nice shape is to make sure the dough is soft enough to pipe, which is where the addition of milk helps. If it's a particularly cold day, you can warm the batter very gently either in short bursts in the microwave or really carefully over a bain-marie. The goal isn't to melt the butter, but just to soften the mixture enough that it can glide smoothly out of the piping bag without breaking. Once you've piped the dough, putting it back in the fridge to set lowers the risk of the biscuits spreading as they bake. Dipping them into chocolate is optional, by the way, you can always eat them as they are. If you prefer a sweeter taste then use milk chocolate instead of dark.

Makes about 25–30

150g unsalted butter, softened
1 tsp vanilla bean paste
pinch of salt
40g icing sugar
175g plain flour
25g cornflour
2 tbsp whole milk
100g dark chocolate, melted, to dip

In a stand mixer, beat the butter with the vanilla and salt until completely smooth and soft.

In a separate bowl, stir together the dry ingredients.

Add the dry ingredients to the butter mixture and mix well until evenly combined. Finally, add the milk and mix in.

The mixture should be a pipeable consistency. If it's too firm, you can *very* gently warm it until soft enough to pipe (see introduction).

Preheat the oven to 160°C fan/ 180°C/gas mark 4 and line two baking trays with baking paper.

Fit a star nozzle (I used 1M) into a piping bag and spoon in the biscuit dough.

Pipe swirls of the mixture in an 'S' shape with an extra tail onto two prepared baking trays, leaving a little space between each one.

Bake for 10–12 minutes until lightly golden. Allow to cool completely on the baking tray.

Dip half of each shortcake swirl into melted chocolate, then place on a tray lined with baking paper. Place in the fridge for 10 minutes until the chocolate has set.

Crunchy Chocolate Sandwich Biscuits

I wanted to make a dark chocolate version of Maryland cookies that stay crunchy and short after baking. These are really cute and last for ages if you keep them in an airtight container (though I highly doubt you will get the chance). They just happen to be vegan, too.

These biscuits are really great eaten on their own and even better sandwiched together with ganache; the combination of this crunchy biscuit with Malt Chocolate Ganache (see page 26) will make your eyes roll back into your head with pleasure.

Makes 30 single biscuits, or 15 sandwich biscuits

80ml neutral oil

1 tbsp golden syrup

70g light brown sugar

4g/scant 1 tsp bicarbonate of soda

small pinch of sea salt flakes

20g cocoa powder

110g plain flour

20g vegan dark chocolate, chopped into small pieces

⅓ quantity Malt Chocolate Ganache (see page 26)

Whisk the oil and golden syrup together in a small bowl.

In a large bowl, mix together the sugar, bicarbonate of soda, salt, cocoa powder and flour. Pour in the oil and syrup and mix until a dough forms, then add in the chopped chocolate, making sure the pieces are really small, and mix well to combine.

Scoop the mixture onto a work surface lined with clingfilm or baking paper and roll into a cylinder shape, roughly 23 x 5cm (9 x 2in). Wrap the cylinder tightly in the clingfilm or baking paper and place on a tray. Refrigerate for 4 hours and then freeze for 2 hours.

When you're ready to bake, preheat the oven to 160°C fan/180°C/ gas mark 4. Line two large baking trays with baking paper.

Using a sharp knife, slice the biscuit dough into 5mm (¼in) slices and place on the prepared trays, leaving plenty of space between each.

Bake for 15 minutes until golden, then allow to cool on the trays before sandwiching with the malt chocolate ganache.

Chees
Chees
Chees
Chees

ecake

ecake ecake

ecake ecake

ecake

One thing I've learned is that 99 per cent of you love cheesecake.

Do you remember the Sara Lee frozen cheesecake? If you don't, then let me enlighten you. It was a popular dessert sold in the frozen aisle of most supermarkets; to eat it you could either microwave it (yes, really) or defrost it in the fridge. The strawberries on top were coated in a gel and, for some reason, always remained slightly icy in the middle. I moved on from the Sara Lee cheesecakes of my early childhood to own-brand supermarket fresh cheesecakes, then to those offered at local Italian restaurants, then to the luxury of Gü cheesecake pots packaged in their own glass ramekins.

When I went to university, despite never being told what I could or couldn't eat, I lost all sense of *how* to eat. In my first year, I shared accommodation with my friends Katie and Chloe, while Nat lived opposite and would join us for dinner most nights. We developed a habit of cheesecake-eating, sampling cheesecakes from all the local supermarkets, fresh and frozen, brand-named or not. And we really got through them.

In fact, while most of our peers were pre-drinking before a big night out, the four of us would get all glammed up, sit in the living room with a fork each and polish off an entire cheesecake. We would then head out and dance for hours… oh, to go back to those days.

At that time, I thought that there was only one way of making a cheesecake: mixing together all the filling ingredients, chucking it on top of some crushed-up buttery digestives and calling it a day. Little did I know that in a few years I would be rushing off to train as a pastry chef, learning about all different types of cheesecake.

There are endless cheesecake possibilities and I urge you to try some of the versions in this chapter. There's one for each mood. One thing I've realized since becoming a pastry chef is that 99 per cent of you **LOVE** cheesecake; that makes me happy because I love cheesecake too. So I thought I should dedicate a bit more time and space to it in this book, giving you a few options, depending on your cheesecake mood.

Japanese Cheesecake

I stood in line for one of these for *ages* a few years back, after a friend raved about them. At this place you could watch the chefs making them and there was a one-hour wait for each small batch. The machines were whipping for a really long time, then the batter was poured into a tin and baked in a bain-marie. The finished result is a cross between a really light, fluffy sponge cake and a cheesecake.

This recipe was avidly tested by my friend Josep Gay-Costa, aka Pep. It is a good recipe for those of you who don't like sweeter desserts, as you can reduce the overall sugar quantity by 30g if you prefer.

While testing this, I found the type of egg you use makes a big difference. I tested with both medium Burford Browns and medium St Ewe's rich yolk eggs. When I tested with the rich yolk eggs, I found that the cheesecake was a lot richer and more custardy in taste and texture. It also looked vividly yellow. When I used the Burford Browns, although the yolk is slightly more orange than regular eggs, the texture was closer to cotton, and what I would imagine a traditional Japanese cheesecake to taste like. So there's my two cents on eggs and how changing the type of egg can change the outcome drastically!

Makes a 20cm (8in) cheesecake

60g unsalted butter, plus extra for the tin

100ml whole milk

1 vanilla pod, split lengthways, seeds scraped out (or 1 tsp vanilla extract)

250g full-fat cream cheese, at room temperature

60g plain flour

15g/1 tbsp cornflour

¼ tsp fine salt

170g caster sugar

6 medium eggs, separated

finely grated zest and juice of ½ unwaxed lemon

¼ tsp cream of tartar

icing sugar, to dust

Preheat the oven to 200°C/gas mark 6 (don't use a fan oven). It's important to use a cake tin that doesn't have a loose bottom; preferably choose a good-quality, deep, non-stick 20cm (8in) tin. Line the base with a circle of baking paper and generously butter the sides.

Gently melt the butter into the milk in a saucepan. Stir in the vanilla seeds or extract, take off the heat and set aside.

Prepare a bain-marie by placing a saucepan of water on the stove and putting a large heatproof bowl on top, making sure the bowl isn't touching the water. Put the cream cheese into the bowl and stir with a whisk until it is smooth and slightly runny.

Stir together the flour, cornflour and salt in a separate bowl.

Remove the cream cheese bowl from the heat and whisk in half the sugar, followed by the egg yolks, then pour in the milk and melted butter. Add the lemon zest and juice.

Japanese Cheesecake

Sift over the dry ingredients and stir with a whisk, making sure there are no lumps. Set aside.

Make a French meringue by placing the cream of tartar into the egg whites in a clean bowl. Whisk until frothy, then add the remaining sugar and whisk until you reach soft peak stage.

Whisk one-third of the meringue into the cream cheese mixture, then gently fold in the rest in two batches. We want to keep this mixture light and delicate, so do not overwork it. When folding, make sure you are constantly touching the bottom of the bowl, as parts will start to settle there if not.

Pour the cheesecake mixture gently into the prepared cake tin.

We bake this in a bain-marie. Boil a kettle full of water. Place a tea towel in a large roasting tin, then put the cheesecake tin directly on top. Slide this into the oven. Pour enough boiling water into the roasting tin to reach halfway up the sides of the cheesecake tin. (Do not keep the oven open for too long, or you will lose a lot of heat.)

Bake for 25 minutes, then reduce the oven temperature to 140°C/gas mark 1 (again, with no fan) and bake for a further 30 minutes. Turn the oven off, leaving the cheesecake inside.

After 20 minutes in the turned-off oven, take the cheesecake out of the bain-marie and immediately remove the cheesecake from its tin by flipping it out onto your hand and then onto a wire cooling rack. Be cautious here: if you are too forceful you will get a hand print in your cheesecake! I have made that mistake a few times – Pep's tip is to turn the cake out onto a small plate before flipping it over onto a wire rack, to avoid that hand print.

Allow to cool fully before dusting with icing sugar.

This cheesecake keeps really well in the fridge, and I think it gets better after a day in there. Serve chilled or at room temperature.

No-Bake White Chocolate Cheesecake with Raspberries

I get asked a lot about egg-free recipes, so here is a fantastic one for you. The first cheesecake I ever made was a no-bake version, and that's kind of how I thought all cheesecakes were made. So while we are keeping it really simple with the filling here, I think it's only right that you make the base!

I've suggested serving this with raspberries; you can, of course, change the accompanying fruit to suit the season.

Makes a 20cm (8in) cheesecake

For the base
½ quantity Baked NY Cheesecake base (see page 60)

For the filling
200g double cream
470g full-fat cream cheese, at room temperature
90g caster sugar
90g soured cream
100g white chocolate, chopped and melted (see page 45)
pinch of sea salt flakes

To serve
150g raspberries
1 tbsp icing sugar, if needed
juice of ½ lemon

Prepare the base of the cheesecake by pressing the baked crumble and melted butter mixture from the food processor into a 20cm (8in) springform tin.

To make the filling, start by whipping the double cream to soft peaks.

In a separate bowl, beat the cream cheese until smooth, then add the sugar and mix in. Add the soured cream and stir until homogeneous.

Allow the melted white chocolate to cool until no longer hot, then stir it into the cream cheese mixture. Finally, fold in the softly whipped cream and salt.

Pour into the prepared tin on top of the base and place in the fridge overnight to set.

Taste the raspberries: when in season at their absolute best, they are sweet and sharp enough not to need any more sugar. However, if yours are sour, feel free to add the 1 tbsp icing sugar. Mash with the lemon juice and serve with the cheesecake.

Baked NY Cheesecake

A crust that slightly absorbs the topping while staying biscuity, and a richly baked cream that you need to spend a bit of time consuming, with a fork; you've got to have a bit of patience with the bake and set on this cheesecake, and you absolutely can't rush it. Traditionally, you would use full-fat soured cream (sour cream), so I tested this recipe with both soured cream and crème fraîche. I found the crème fraîche gave a creamier, silkier texture, but if you only have soured cream to hand, that's also cool!

I like to serve mine with 250g strawberries, halved and tossed in lemon juice with 1 tsp caster sugar.

The base ingredients here make enough for two cheesecake bases, but it's not worth making only half, so I always make a full batch and freeze half.

Makes a 20cm (8in) cheesecake (with enough mix for two bases; I always freeze half)

For the base

160g plain flour

25g caster sugar

25g dark brown sugar

¼ tsp ground cinnamon

¼ tsp ground ginger

¼ tsp fine salt

¼ tsp bicarbonate of soda

112g unsalted butter, chilled and cubed, plus 60g unsalted butter, melted

40g golden syrup

For the filling

680g full-fat cream cheese, at room temperature

150g caster sugar

1 vanilla pod, split lengthways, seeds scraped out

pinch of fine salt

finely grated zest and juice of ½ unwaxed lemon

3 eggs, 1 yolk

1½ tbsp cornflour

120g double cream

200g full-fat crème fraîche

strawberries or other seasonal fruit, to serve (optional)

Preheat the oven to 160°C fan/180°C/gas mark 4.

Mix together all the dry ingredients for the base. Add the chilled cubed butter and mix to the texture of loose breadcrumbs. Drizzle in the syrup and mix until a dough forms. Freeze half for your next cheesecake.

Crumble the remaining base mixture into a baking tray in a single layer and bake for 25–30 minutes, stirring the edges into the middle a couple of times so it browns evenly. The crumble should be golden and cooked throughout.

Remove from the oven and allow to cool. Blitz the crumble in a food processor to re-crumble it, then stir in the melted butter.

Increase the oven temperature to 180°C fan/200°C/gas mark 6.

Line the base and sides of a 20cm (8in) cake tin with baking paper. Press the base into the prepared tin. You can line the base alone, or bring some up the sides.

Bake for 10 minutes, then allow to cool while you make the filling. Leave the oven on.

Beat the cream cheese gently in a stand mixer fitted with the paddle attachment (or in a large bowl with a wooden spoon) until softened, then add the sugar and beat slowly to combine. Add the vanilla seeds, salt and lemon zest. Add the eggs and egg yolk to the bowl and beat slowly until thoroughly mixed.

In a separate bowl, gradually add the cornflour to the double cream while stirring with a whisk to ensure there are no lumps. Add the crème fraîche and stir until smooth. Add this mixture, along with the lemon juice, to the cream cheese mixture and stir to combine. Pour into the prepared cake tin over the base.

Put the cake tin on a baking tray and place on the middle shelf of the oven. Bake for 10 minutes.

Reduce the oven temperature to 130°C fan/150°C/gas mark 3 and bake for a further 1 hour 10 minutes, or until the middle is very slightly jiggly and the edges are set. Turn the oven off and leave the cheesecake to cool in the oven for 4 hours. When it is at room temperature, place it in the fridge to set for a minimum of 6 hours.

Slice and eat on its own, or with seasonal fruit. It will keep for 3–4 days in the fridge, though the base will gradually become more soggy, so keep that in mind.

Basque Cheesecake

This is so low-fuss it's unbelievable, perfect for anyone who is short on time and needs to make something quick (preferably for the next day). It is a caramelized cheesecake, baked high and fast, that can be eaten warm or served the next day straight from the fridge. I think it gets better and better day by day to be honest. You'll love me for this.

Makes a 20cm (8in) cheesecake

650g full-fat cream cheese, at room temperature
300g caster sugar
5 eggs
150g soured cream
230g double cream
35g cornflour
3g/½ tsp sea salt flakes

Preheat the oven to 220°C/gas mark 7, without the fan running.

In the bowl of a stand mixer, or in a large bowl with a wooden spoon, beat the cream cheese until soft and pliable. Add the sugar and beat until fully mixed. Add the eggs, one at a time, beating well between each addition.

In a separate bowl, stir together the soured cream and double cream.

In another (small) bowl, mix the cornflour and salt together, then stir this through the creams, before adding to the cream cheese mixture. Beat well.

Line a 20cm (8in) baking tin with a piece of baking paper, large enough to line the base and come right up over the edges. Use a bowl to hold it in place while you cut another large piece of baking paper. Lay the second sheet the opposite way on top, forming a cross with the first piece so the tin is completely covered with paper. You want the paper coming over the top of the tin, as this will help you to lift the baked cheesecake out. It's important that there are no holes in the paper lining, as this would cause the mix to leak and make a mess in the bottom of the oven.

Make sure the paper is securely in place, then pour the cheesecake mixture into the tin. Put the tin on a baking tray and place in the middle of the oven.

Bake for 45–50 minutes until dark on top and puffy. It might crack a little around the edges, which is fine. It should be jiggly in the middle, though.

Remove from the oven and serve warm, or allow to cool completely before placing in the fridge overnight (this will lend a perfectly creamy texture). The next day, cut and serve.

Mango Cheesecake Tart

I wanted to make something with the freshness of a mango and the silkiness of a baked cheesecake. This filling is so rich and yet refreshing at the same time; it works really nicely with the burned caramel flavour on top, which you get once it is brûléed.

Start by making the pastry, giving it enough time to rest in the fridge before rolling; chilling pastry is the key to achieving that beautiful shell.

This pastry will make enough for two tarts, so wrap the leftover tightly and freeze it ready to use another time. Fill just to the top of the tart case; if you have any extra mix, don't be tempted to pour it all in.

Makes a 20cm (8in) tart (with enough dough for two pastry bases, I always freeze half)

For the pastry

230g plain flour, plus extra for dusting

90g icing sugar

30g ground almonds

2g/½ tsp fine salt

finely grated zest of 1 lime

120g unsalted butter, cubed

1 egg, plus 1 egg, lightly beaten, to brush

For the filling

420g full-fat cream cheese, at room temperature

2 eggs, lightly beaten

50g soured cream

120ml mango purée

juice of 1 lime

110g caster sugar, plus 30g extra for the brûléed topping

18g plain flour

70g double cream

2g/½ tsp fine salt

Stir together all the dry ingredients for the pastry and add the lime zest.

Mix the cold cubed butter into the flour mixture, either by using the paddle attachment in a stand mixer, pulsing in a food processor or rubbing into crumbs with your hands. Mix until the butter is no longer visible. Add the egg and work together quickly and gently until a loose dough forms.

Turn out onto a work surface and bring together with your hands, then pat down into a disc. Cut the disc evenly in half and wrap both halves in clingfilm. Freeze one to use another time and chill the other in the fridge for a minimum of 4 hours.

Roll the chilled pastry out to a thickness of 4mm (¼in) on a lightly floured work surface. Line a 20cm (8in) tart case with the chilled pastry, then chill in the fridge for 1 hour. You will have some leftover pastry after trimming, keep it wrapped up in clingfilm and save for the future.

Preheat the oven to 160°C fan/180°C/gas mark 4. Line the pastry case with baking paper, fill with baking beans and bake for 30 minutes until the edges are golden. Remove the baking beans and paper and bake for a further 10 minutes.

Brush the pastry case with the beaten egg to seal and flash in the oven for a further 4 minutes.

Reduce the oven temperature to 150°C fan/170°C/gas mark 3½.

For the filling, beat the cream cheese until softened and not lumpy, then gradually add the eggs, soured cream, mango purée and lime juice, beating after each addition and scraping down the sides of the bowl as you go. Add the 110g of sugar and mix in.

In a separate bowl, whisk the flour and double cream together, then add this to the cream cheese mixture with the salt. Mix until silky and smooth.

Pour the cheesecake filling right to the top of the pastry case and bake for 40–45 minutes, discard any leftover filling. The middle should still have a slight jiggle when removed.

Allow to cool at room temperature (this is very important) before placing in the fridge to chill for 4 hours.

Brûlée the top with the remaining 30g caster sugar before enjoying: sprinkle half in an even layer on top of the tart, wiping any off the pastry. Brûlée with a blowtorch or under a scorching-hot grill, keeping an eye on it so that it doesn't burn. Allow to cool, then repeat, for a thick and crunchy layer.

This tart keeps in the fridge for 3 days, but the pastry will not be as crisp as the days go on.

Rhubarb and Orange Cheesecake

I used to do an event at Llewelyn's, a neighbourhood restaurant in Herne Hill, called 'Cheesecake Fridays'. I loved channelling the seasons through the medium of cheesecake: what a joyous way to live and work! One of our biggest hits was this cheesecake; I think it's the visual contrast between forced, beautifully bright pink rhubarb and white cheesecake filling. The gentle warm spicing from the base against the cold, slightly zingy sour rhubarb, and then the creamy filling, come together to create complete oral satisfaction. Enough to hit the sides of your cheeks and leave you wanting to eat the entire cake (if you're anything like me before a night out).

A NOTE: This cheesecake does not work without gelatine or its vegetarian alternatives (check the package instructions to work out the quantity conversion).

Rhubarb and Orange Cheesecake

Makes a 20cm (8in) cheesecake

For the base

½ quantity Baked NY Cheesecake base (see page 60)

For the filling

5 'platinum-grade' gelatine leaves (I use Dr. Oetker)

110g caster sugar

40ml water, plus extra if needed

1 egg and 1 egg yolk

finely grated zest of 1 orange and juice of ½

juice of 1 lemon

340g full-fat cream cheese, at room temperature

320g double cream, lightly whipped

For the roasted rhubarb and jelly

150g forced rhubarb

90g caster sugar

100ml water, plus extra if needed

juice of 1 orange, plus extra if needed

1 'platinum-grade' gelatine leaf (I use Dr. Oetker), or as needed

Make the base of the cheesecake by pressing the baked crumble and butter mixture from the food processor into a 20cm (8in) springform tin.

For the filling, we have to start by making a *pâté à bombe,* by pouring hot sugar over whipped egg yolks.

Soak the gelatine in a bowl of ice-cold water.

Put the sugar in a small saucepan with the measured water, add a thermometer and heat to 119°C.

Meanwhile, start whipping the egg and egg yolk on a medium speed in a stand mixer. As it's such a small amount, make sure the whisk is touching the bottom of the bowl, because it's essential to get some volume into these eggs before the sugar is added, it helps to achieve a beautifully light-textured cheesecake. Whisk until pale and thick.

Pour the hot sugar syrup slowly down the side of the bowl as the machine is whisking, ensuring that the stream does not touch the whisk. The hot sugar will 'cook' the egg yolks. Let this whisk on a medium speed until the bowl is no longer hot to touch.

Pour the orange and lemon juice into the same pan that the sugar was heated in. Heat it gently, but do not boil, then squeeze out the excess water from the gelatine before dissolving it in the juice. When the gelatine has dissolved (it takes seconds) remove from the heat and add to the pâté à bombe. Whisk it in gently.

In a separate bowl, beat the cream cheese until smooth and add to the pâté à bombe mixture. Mix until completely smooth. Fold in the lightly whipped cream and orange zest.

Pour the filling over the base and refrigerate overnight.

The next day, make the roasted rhubarb topping. Preheat the oven to 150°C fan/170°C/gas mark 3½.

Cut the rhubarb into 5cm (2in) pieces and toss them in the sugar, measured water and orange juice. Spread out on a baking tray in a single even layer and roast for 10–15 minutes. The sugar should melt, leaving a syrup on the tray, and the rhubarb should be tender, not mushy; it should still hold its shape when prodded. Take out of the oven and allow to cool at room temperature.

Strain the rhubarb cooking liquid into a measuring jug; set the roasted rhubarb aside. Weigh the cooking liquid and taste it. We are aiming for 100ml of liquid to cover the top of the cheesecake and you need 1 sheet to set that amount. This is very important: if it's flat, add some acidity in the form of extra orange juice, and if it's too sweet, add a bit more water to dilute it. This will be poured and set on top of the cheesecake.

To make the jelly, soak the gelatine in a bowl of ice-cold water.

Warm the rhubarb cooking liquid gently in a small saucepan. Squeeze out the gelatine leaf and stir in until dissolved. Don't heat the liquid for too long, or you risk losing the colour.

Take off the heat and cool slightly, then pour over the cheesecake and return to the fridge to set. As it's thin, this should only take 30 minutes.

To serve, remove the cheesecake from the tin and slice. Serve with the roasted rhubarb and prepare to be orally satisfied. And if it all gets too much and you eat the whole thing while staring into space, pop on a pair of trousers with an elasticated waistband and paint the town red.

weet
ughs
sweet
ughs

The pastry section was a bit like a confessional.

Whenever I've worked in a restaurant kitchen with a counter offering, I've always loved coming up with new sweet dough options. Yeasted doughs used to scare me, and the subject does not tend to be covered widely at cookery school. Yeast can be quite the variable: your results can change depending on the weather, the other ingredients in the recipe or even the kitchen environment.

I'm not going to lie to you: professional kitchens can be really – shall we say – testing for your strength of character. Early on in my career, I would crumble at any ounce of confrontation. I just couldn't handle it. I took everything personally and felt constantly on edge. My thoughts are with anyone else who has shed a secret tear or two in the walk-in fridge or dry store, before quickly wiping them away with some blue roll and heading right back into the thick of it.

You see, I quickly learned that, in order to progress, I had to appear as though I had it together on the outside, to my friends, colleagues, bosses and family. When really inside I was soft and very insecure. Sort of like a sweet bun (minus the insecurity, I suppose, but I don't know, I've never asked). One of the things I love most about working as a pastry chef in a big kitchen is being able to tuck myself away into a corner in a sweet world of my own.

Sometimes, chefs would describe me as weaker for being in the pastry section. And I get it, we don't sear off joints of meat, butcher whole animals, kill lobsters or chop onions at light speed, sweating under the pressure of the many pots on the go. But our battle still exists, it's just different. Sometimes the heat of the kitchen means your chocolate shards won't temper, or someone moving your trays of dough to a colder part of the kitchen to get them out of the way might mean that you don't get them proved and baked in time. And often, if you work in pastry, you're the first one in – working to get your doughs proved – and the last one out, after making sure the last customer got to decide whether they wanted dessert or not at 11pm on a Tuesday night.

I think a gentle hand and an understanding of touch and feel can really help anyone to get to grips with yeasted dough. Especially when it comes to knowing when it's just right and ready to go. It takes a lot of time and practice. I think the same is true for how we understand each other: it requires a level of openness and acceptance. A conscious effort not to judge each other for where we are or where we're going. For we were all once at a stage of not knowing our way; we all have to learn it from someone or something else.

Funnily enough, I always felt as if the pastry section in a big kitchen was a bit like a confessional. You'd attract people from all parts of the kitchen over with sweet, welcoming, comforting smells. Something about that fragrance makes people tell you their secrets. It's weird, isn't it? (There is, of course, a rule of absolute discretion and a no-judgement clause.)

Throughout the day, different people would appear asking for a sugar hit while swapping me a coffee and simultaneously venting about their day in the quickest three-minute burst. You'd soon find out who was banging who – knowing the other person had just told you about someone else they liked – who had got drunk the night before and behaved badly, who was getting the most tips, or the latest on the dramas of the regular customers. It goes on. I would find that a lot of the male chefs with the biggest bravado would come and ask me for advice on who they were dating and so on. Getting the ovens on early to bake that sweet dough, getting the aromas going through the kitchen from early doors, appears to be a good way of providing comfort to those around you.

It's as if that sweet smell in the pastry corner relaxes people and helps them put their guard down. Just for a split second though, before – **SNAP** – it all goes back to normal.

The Brioche Cube

I ran a string of pop-ups called PUFF with the help of some friends, back at the start of 2020 before COVID hit. The name originated back to my St. JOHN days, when I would fantasize about opening a bakery that only sold things that were 'puffed up' and I would draw cloud logos on the steel walls with dry wipe pens. The pop-ups were wild and enabled me to experiment, making the sweet stuff of my dreams (and more than just puff and choux), using local suppliers, without the worry of overheads. During this time, we started selling these little and large cubes of brioche filled with custard. This is how the idea was conceived, over a WhatsApp conversation, which I think will give you a valuable insight into my working process:

'WHAT IF...
We baked a perfect CUBE of brioche
Then coated and rolled it in a crunch sugar
Then
Piped it full of mousseline...
D*MN'

And that's how it was born. It was really funny watching people lose their minds over them. We would have queues round the block for an hour and a half before the doors opened, just to try these brioche cubes, baked and filled (with custard in the end, not mousseline).
Here's how to make them at home.

The Brioche Cube

**Makes 9 small cubes prepared
in a silicone tray measuring
40 x 19 x 5cm (16 x 7.5 x 2in)**

For the brioche

230g strong white bread flour, plus
  extra for dusting

½ tsp fine salt

15g/1 tbsp caster sugar, plus 30g
  for brûléeing the tops

4g/scant 1 tsp fast-action dried
  yeast

3 eggs

10g/2 tsp honey

150g unsalted butter, softened

neutral oil, for oiling

For the custard

350ml whole milk

1 vanilla pod, split lengthways,
  seeds scraped out

300g double cream

85g caster sugar

45g cornflour

3 egg yolks, plus 1 egg, lightly
  beaten together

30g caster sugar, for brûléeing

To make the brioche, combine the flour, salt and 15g/1 tbsp sugar in the bowl of a stand mixer fitted with a dough hook and stir together well.

Add the yeast, eggs and honey. Mix on a medium speed until a dough forms, then continue to mix until the dough is smooth. Turn the machine off and let the dough relax for 5 minutes.

Turn the machine back on to a medium speed and gradually add the softened butter until combined. Allow to mix for 10–15 minutes, until the dough is smooth, shiny and elastic.

Transfer the dough to a work surface and 'slap and fold' it 4–5 times. Do this by slapping half the dough down and folding the other half over it, then pick it all up, rotate by 90° and repeat.

Place the dough in a large, oiled bowl, cover and refrigerate overnight.

The next day, remove the dough from the fridge and knock it down gently in the bowl.

Transfer to a lightly floured work surface and roll out gently to a 15cm (6in) square, 2.5cm (1in) deep. Cut out 9 squares and place them neatly in a square silicone mould. Cover with a damp tea towel and prove at room temperature for 1 hour until soft and risen.

Preheat the oven to 180°C fan/200°C/gas mark 6.

To bake, place the silicone mould on a baking tray, place a piece of baking paper on top of the mould and place another tray directly on top. This pressure will force the brioche into its iconic cube shape.

Bake for 10 minutes, then reduce the oven temperature to 160°C fan/180°C/gas mark 4 and bake for a further 8 minutes.

Remove from the mould and allow to cool.

For the custard, gently heat the milk, vanilla and half the double cream with half the sugar in a saucepan.

Meanwhile, in a bowl, mix the rest of the sugar with the cornflour, then whisk this into the yolks and whole egg until pale and slightly fluffy.

When the milk mixture is just about to come to the boil, pour the hot liquid over the egg mix in 3–4 batches, whisking well after each addition. Return this to the pan over a medium heat.

Stir the mixture with a whisk until it starts thickening, then whisk faster until it starts bubbling. Take it off the heat for a moment while whisking if you need to take back the control, but you'll need it to bubble while you whisk it over the heat for at least 1–2 minutes, so it cooks.

Remove from the heat and immediately whisk in the remaining cream. Use a spatula to pour the custard into a bowl or onto a tray so it cools faster. Cover with clingfilm directly touching the surface.

If it's a bit lumpy and you're not happy with it, use a hand blender to knock out those lumps once it has cooled.

Make a small hole in the base of each cube with the tip of a round piping nozzle and pipe the custard in.

Now, to brûlée the tops of the cubes: sprinkle half of the 30g of caster sugar in an even layer on top of the cubes. Brûlée with a blowtorch or under a scorching-hot grill, keeping an eye on them so they don't burn. Allow to cool, then repeat, for a thick and crunchy layer.

You will have some custard leftover – just eat it!

Devonshire Splits

These are so quintessentially British and I'm not quite sure why they don't make more of an appearance in bakeries, because they are such a great teatime snack. I made these at St. JOHN during my time there and Fergus Henderson was a big fan. They are a great way of showing off well-made jam and local cream (if you can source it).

Makes 12

For the buns

100ml whole milk
200ml water
7g/1½ tsp fast-action dried yeast
450g strong white bread flour
20g caster sugar
5g/1 tsp fine salt
15g/1 tbsp milk powder
50g unsalted butter, softened
neutral oil, for oiling
1 egg, lightly beaten

To serve

200g double cream
10g/2 tsp caster sugar
generous amounts of seasonal jam
icing sugar, for dusting

Mix the milk and measured water together and heat very gently and slowly in a pan until just warm to the touch. Sprinkle in the yeast and stir.

Mix the strong white flour, sugar, salt and milk powder together in the bowl of a stand mixer fitted with a dough hook. Pour the milk mixture over the dry ingredients and mix on a medium speed for 10 minutes. Turn the power off and cover the bowl with a tea towel for 5 minutes.

Add the softened butter to the bowl and mix on a medium-slow speed until incorporated. Increase the speed to medium and mix to develop the dough and give it strength. The dough should be smooth, silky and elastic.

Lightly oil a large bowl. Scoop the dough out of the machine onto a work surface and shape it into a smooth ball. Pop into the oiled bowl, cover with a damp tea towel and leave to double in size (1–2 hours).

When the dough has doubled, press it down in the bowl, then tip out and divide into 70g portions. Roll each of these into balls.

Place the dough balls on a baking tray, spacing them out enough so that they won't touch each other when growing and baking. Lightly oil the tops and cover with a tea towel, then set aside until puffy and light (around 25 minutes).

Preheat the oven to 180°C fan/200°C/gas mark 6.

Gently brush the tops of the buns with the beaten egg and bake for 12–15 minutes until golden. Remove from the oven and allow to cool.

Whip the cream to soft peaks with the caster sugar.

Slice each bun through the middle and fill with the lightly sweetened whipped cream and a dollop of jam. Finally, dust with icing sugar (optional). These are best eaten on the same day that they are baked.

Prune and Chocolate Buns

I made these during my time at St. JOHN restaurant and they were sold on the counter to anyone lucky enough to arrive in time.

Makes 6 large buns

For the buns

375g strong white bread flour, plus extra for dusting

30g caster sugar

3g/½ tsp fine salt

1 egg

155ml whole milk

7g/1½ tsp fast-action dried yeast

100g unsalted butter, softened, plus more for greasing

For the filling

60g unsalted butter

90g caster sugar

50g dark chocolate, chopped

20g cocoa powder

generous pinch of sea salt flakes

40g roasted hazelnuts (see page 191), chopped

8–9 juicy prunes, smushed

For the sugar syrup

140g caster sugar

130ml water

2–3 tbsp armagnac (optional)

Mix the flour, sugar and salt in the bowl of a stand mixer fitted with a dough hook. In a separate bowl, whisk the egg into the milk.

Sprinkle the yeast onto the flour mixture and stir in, then pour in the egg mixture. Mix together until a rough dough forms. Add the softened butter and mix on a medium speed until a smooth dough forms, roughly 5 minutes. This dough will not be super-elastic, instead it will look enriched, smooth and pliable.

Place in a buttered container, cover and put in the fridge overnight.

For the filling, melt the butter in a saucepan over a low heat, then remove from the heat and stir in the sugar, followed by the chocolate. Stir until melted, then add the cocoa powder and salt. Set aside at room temperature.

Roll out the dough to 4mm (¼in) thick, roughly 32.5 x 28cm (13 x 11in), on a lightly floured work surface. Spread over the chocolate filling and then scatter over the hazelnuts and smushed prunes.

Roll the dough up lengthways, tightly. Trim the ends if they are messy, then cut into 6 even pieces, each roughly 5cm (2in). Arrange, cut-sides up, in a 20cm (8in) cake tin lined with baking paper. Cover with a damp tea towel and leave to prove until the buns have doubled in size.

Preheat the oven to 180°C fan/200°C/gas mark 6. Remove the tea towel and bake for 10 minutes, then reduce the oven temperature to 160°C fan/180°C/gas mark 4 and bake for a further 20 minutes until golden.

Meanwhile, for the syrup, boil the sugar and measured water together for a few minutes. Set aside. If adding armagnac, do it just before using.

When the buns are out of the oven, leave them to rest for 10 minutes before pouring the sugar syrup evenly on top and leaving it to absorb and soak in. Remove from the tin when cooled and eat. These are best served on the day they are baked.

Roasted Grape Focaccia (Schiacciata All'uva)

A few years ago, I had the pleasure of working with a talented pastry chef called Jennifer Moseley at a beautiful place called Wild by Tart. This company was started by Lucy Carr-Ellison and Jemima Jones, two wonderful women and business partners who have some of the cleanest hearts in the food world. They have an amazing vision and are always open to new ideas, never feeling restricted when it comes to food. I worked with them to develop a sweet offering and loved the creative freedom they gave me as well as their input; we learned from each other and it was a really fabulous way to work.

Jennifer became the head of pastry when the restaurant opened and together we developed the sweet menu and brought together a team of fantastic pastry chefs.

One of the best things Jen introduced me to was a sweet focaccia with stout-roasted grapes dusted liberally with icing sugar. It was so good that I would always ask for the offcuts to take home at the end of a shift. The best time to make this is in September, when the right grapes are in season, however, you can forego this, as I'm sure most of you will, and just use the best dark grapes that you can lay your hands on. Jen starts by roasting the grapes in stout and, trust me on this, they are so good that you will want to put them on more than just this focaccia.

Makes a 35 x 25cm (14 x 10in) tray

For the focaccia

600g strong white bread flour

12g/2½ tsp fine salt

9g/2 tsp fresh yeast, or 3g/½ tsp fast-action dried yeast

6ml/1 tsp olive oil, plus extra for oiling

400ml water

75g demerara sugar

3–4 rosemary sprigs

icing sugar, for dusting

For the stout-roasted grapes

560g seedless red grapes

35g demerara sugar

300ml Guinness, or any stout

1 tbsp pomegranate molasses

Mix together the flour and salt in the bowl of a stand mixer fitted with a dough hook. Add the yeast and stir in.

Mix in the olive oil and measured water on a medium-low speed until a dough forms. Increase the mixer speed to medium and mix for 6–7 minutes, until the dough is smooth and elastic.

Lightly oil a large bowl, then place the dough in the bowl and cover with a tea towel or clingfilm. Leave in a warm place to prove until double in size; 1–2 hours. Or alternatively, place in the fridge overnight and use chilled the following morning (if using this latter method you will need to prove it for longer once the grapes have been added).

To roast the grapes, preheat the oven to 170°C fan/190°C/gas mark 5.

Remove the grapes from the vine and place in a roasting tin. Sprinkle over the sugar, stout and pomegranate molasses, mix together and roast for 30 minutes, or until they look like they've taken on the flavours and have plumped up ready to burst.

Line a baking tray with baking paper, or use a really good-quality non-stick baking tin oiled very, very well.

Divide the focaccia dough in half. Stretch out half in the prepared tray. Sprinkle over half each of the grapes and demerara sugar.

Stretch the second half of the focaccia dough over the top. Gently push the second half of the grapes into the dough, followed by the rosemary. Finish by sprinkling with the remaining demerara sugar.

Cover the tray with clingfilm or a tea towel and prove at room temperature until doubled in size again.

Preheat the oven to 200°C fan/220°C/gas mark 7 and bake for 10 minutes, then reduce the oven temperature to 170°C fan/190°C/gas mark 5 and bake for a further 15 minutes.

To serve, sprinkle the top with icing sugar, slice and eat.

Cheese and Jam Buns

This is a really beautiful enriched dough. It's quite straightforward to whip up and so tasty that you will want to keep returning to the tray to eat more.

Makes 8–9

360g strong white bread flour

60g caster sugar

½ tsp fine salt

50ml double cream

150ml whole milk

12g/2½ tsp fast-action dried yeast

1 egg, plus 1 extra, beaten, for brushing

40g unsalted butter, softened

neutral oil, for oiling

250g strong mature Cheddar, cut into 25–30g portions

100g crabapple jelly, or other jam of your choice

In the bowl of a stand mixer fitted with a dough hook, mix together the flour, half the sugar and the salt.

In a small saucepan, gently heat the cream and milk until just warm to the touch. Remove from the heat and stir in the remaining sugar and the yeast. Set aside for 5 minutes.

Pour the yeast and milk mixture over the dry ingredients in the stand mixer and add the egg.

Mix on a medium speed until a dough forms. Occasionally scrape down the bowl and dough hook, too, to help everything mix together.

When a dough has formed, turn the machine off for 5 minutes and allow the dough to relax.

Add the butter and mix on a medium speed until fully incorporated, then keep mixing until the dough becomes smooth and slightly elastic (10–15 minutes).

Cheese and Jam Buns

Oil a large bowl and scrape the dough into the bowl. Cover with a damp tea towel, then leave to prove at room temperature until doubled in size (1½–2 hours).

When the dough has doubled in size, line a large baking tray with baking paper.

Divide the dough into 8–9 even portions, shape each into a ball and place on the prepared tray. Cover with a damp tea towel and leave to prove again for 20–30 minutes.

Preheat the oven to 180°C fan/200°C/gas mark 6.

To bake, using your thumb, make an indent in the middle of each bun and insert 25–30g cheese into each, gently pushing it down. Brush the buns with beaten egg all over.

Bake for 12–14 minutes, until golden, then allow to cool for 5 minutes. Top each bun with a spoonful of jam or jelly and enjoy warm.

Batter-Style Waffles

I like to serve these really simply with extra butter slapped on top, or maple syrup, if I've got the nice stuff around. But as always, do as you please. You can switch the melted butter here for brown butter (see page 30), to add even more flavour.

Makes 7–8 large waffles

For the waffles

200g plain flour

40g caster sugar

8g/1½ tsp baking powder

3g/½ tsp fine salt

finely grated zest of 2 unwaxed lemons

200ml whole milk

2 eggs

340g crème fraîche

80g unsalted butter, melted and cooled slightly

For the optional extras

100g blueberries or other berries

nibbed sugar

chocolate chips

In a large bowl, stir together all the dry ingredients and the lemon zest using a whisk.

In a separate bowl, whisk together all the wet ingredients.

Add the wet ingredients to the dry ingredients and mix well with the whisk. Let the batter rest at room temperature while you heat up the waffle machine.

You can add blueberries or other berries, nibbed sugar and/or even chocolate chips to the batter at this point.

Cook the waffles in a waffle press according to the manufacturer's instructions and enjoy warm.

These also work really well reheated in a toaster.

Liege Waffles

These will impress anyone that you might have loitering in your house ready for breakfast...

Liege waffles are made using a dough as their base rather than a batter. After proving in the fridge overnight, you knead the dough with nibbed sugar, which gives them an amazing flavour and colour when cooking.

Makes 6

1 tbsp golden caster sugar
¼ tsp fine salt
215g plain flour
3g/generous ½ tsp fast-action dried yeast
1 egg
10g/2 tsp clear honey
120ml semi-skimmed milk
50g unsalted butter, softened
neutral oil, for oiling
60g nibbed sugar

In the bowl of a stand mixer fitted with a dough hook, combine the golden caster sugar, salt and flour. Stir well, then add the yeast.

In a separate bowl, mix together the egg, honey and milk. Pour this into the stand mixer and mix for 10 minutes on a medium speed.

Add the butter and mix for a further 10 minutes on a medium speed until fully incorporated.

Turn the dough out onto a lightly oiled work surface and form into a smooth ball, then transfer to an oiled bowl. Cover with clingfilm and refrigerate overnight.

The next day, warm up the waffle machine!

Take the dough and divide it into 6 equal portions. Mix 8g/scant 2 tsp of nibbed sugar into each portion, then form into balls. Place the balls on a lightly oiled plate.

Squish them individually into the waffle press and cook for 5 minutes, or according to the manufacturer's instructions.

Enjoy while still warm with a fruit compote of your choice (see page 149), honey, butter, maple syrup or jam.

You can also wrap these tightly in clingfilm or store in a freezer bag after pressing and cooling. Simply defrost in the toaster to revive.

Brunsviger with Cardamom, Pecan and Sesame

This is a Danish bread introduced to me by Marie Frank, a talented pastry chef from Copenhagen. When I was visiting her city, I saw brunsviger for sale all over the city and was quite intrigued by it, so I asked her how to make it. It's dimpled on top and darkly golden and bread-like underneath. I have added pecans and sesame to the top, as I think it gives a nice texture to this fluffy bread.

After the bread has proved in the tray, you need to poke holes in it and pour over the hot sticky topping before baking. This bread is best eaten warm on the same day that it is baked.

Makes a 18cm x 28cm x 5xm tray (7in x 11in x 2in)

For the bread

500g strong white bread flour

10g/2 tsp fine salt

1 tsp caster sugar

50g fresh yeast, or 15g/1 tbsp fast-action dried yeast

50g unsalted butter, melted

400ml buttermilk

For the sweet topping

150g unsalted butter

150g dark brown sugar

2 tbsp maple syrup

25g runny honey

4 cardamom pods, crushed (with their shells, just blitz the pods)

1 tsp ground cinnamon

finely grated zest of 2 unwaxed lemons

50g pecans

20g sesame seeds

Mix all the dry ingredients for the bread together in a large bowl, then crumble or scatter over the yeast.

Melt the butter and slightly warm the buttermilk in two separate saucepans, then mix them together off the heat. Pour into the dry ingredients and mix to form a dough.

Stretch and press the dough into a 28cm (11in) greased baking tray, cover with a damp tea towel and leave to prove until doubled in size.

Preheat the oven to 200°C fan/220°C/gas mark 7.

For the sweet topping, gently melt the butter, sugar, maple syrup and honey together in a saucepan. Add the spices and lemon zest and mix well. Allow to cool to room temperature.

Poke deep indents all over the dough with your fingers – the important bit! Pour over the sweet topping, which will collect in all the indents, then sprinkle with pecans and sesame seeds.

Bake for 12–15 minutes, then reduce the oven temperature to 180°C fan/200°C/gas mark 6 and cook for a further 10 minutes. Leave to cool in the pan and enjoy while still warm.

T

T

Fried
nings
Fried
nings

There is something about deep-frying that makes me very happy.

It's as though you know that deep-fried food is going to be good just by the pure idea of the hot oil. When I worked one of my very first kitchen jobs, I was on a kitchen island serving up dessert with a chef named Pablo directly opposite me on the fry section. I hated that job, though watching Pablo was always very entertaining as he was extremely erratic and constantly 'going down' (drowning in orders), despite having been on the section for years. Every now and then I'd sneak him a chocolate fondant wrapped in a towel and he would shove a bowl of salt and pepper squid into my hands under the counter.

One of the things I loved the most about Pablo was his willingness to deep-fry anything. Depending on who was watching, I would grab something from my section, throw it to him and mouth 'fry it!', he always did. We would laugh at some of the results and eat most of them. He was definitely not allowed to do this and it probably contributed to him 'going down' most days, but it was fun while it lasted.

Lessons learned from my fry experiments with Pablo:

• No, you cannot simply fry something wet and frozen. It needs to be encased in something else in order for it to work.
• Fruit shouldn't go into the fryer naked, neither should chocolate. You can still eat it, but it's not nice.
• Deep-fried biscuits are silly.
• A lychee or a grape will likely explode. Don't do it.

After moving on from this job I wasn't as lucky to be positioned opposite the fryer section. But that didn't keep me away – a lot of chefs knew about my fondness for chips, so would always keep extras in a bowl on the side during service for me.

I even briefly found work in a fried chicken shop in Soho with my friend Tom; here I would spend my days dredging chicken in batter before lifting the baskets into the pressure fryer, cleaning (constantly scrubbing grease off something) or using long metal tongs to fill up the hot boxes with chicken. When I worked at an Indian restaurant, being positioned in the savoury section meant frying a lot of chilli squid, folding hundreds of samosas and mixing lots of aloo tikki mix.

I then ended up working in a restaurant briefly where the same Tom was head chef. One day Tom had made two gastro trays worth of the most awful undercooked raw banana cake, and, to hide his mistake, he told us he was going to blow our minds by turning it into a deep-fried ice cream sandwich. Tom went ahead and grabbed a tub of shop-bought ice cream and spread it across one of the cake layers before placing the other on top. With all of us watching, Tom then sliced the cake into long strips, dipped it in some batter and deep-fried it. He told us to get ready for one of the most mind-blowing things we'd ever see. We stood back, waiting, and then, after a few minutes, peering over to look into the fryer and realizing what had happened, we all started howling. Tom lifted the fryer basket up to find two strips of densely raw, deep-fried bits of banana bread, with no sign of the ice cream, as it had dissolved into the fryer. I still have an imprint in my mind of Tom trying fiercely to defend his idea and then attempting to eat it out of the fryer whilst simultaneously realizing he was burning his mouth.

The deep fat fryer, I love you, I don't always enjoy cleaning you but I enjoy your results. This chapter is inspired by my love of all things fried and my fleeting relationship with Pablo and his willingness to fry anything.

Simple Sugar Ring Doughnuts

I'm a sucker for cheap sugared doughnuts. At my university prom, while everyone else was getting smashed, I was preoccupied with making sure I timed my evening well enough to buy a bag of hot doughnuts from the stall outside the nightclub before it got too busy. I really am that girl.

My icon, my Biji, also has a love for doughnuts and all things deep-fried: chips, pakoras, samosas, anything really. During the recipe testing of these doughnuts, Biji would wake up from her naps just because she could smell something being fried. We sat and ate these together during a recipe testing day and she told me the same story she does every time she eats a doughnut. It's like that Marcel Proust madeleine moment for her, except just a touch less elegant.

When she moved to this country from Kenya in the 1970s, Biji started work in a sewing factory in Aldgate, East London. A young male worker who called her 'Auntie' started telling her about these sweet buns that English people eat. She had never heard of them, so he bought her a box, some covered in sugar and others filled with jam. They cost roughly 10p and were probably from a Percy Ingle store. Still, to her, they are the best doughnuts she has ever had. A sweet memory (although she reminds me of that 10p box of doughnuts every time I come home with some from a bakery that charges up to £4 for one).

Makes ten 13cm (5in) ring doughnuts

440g strong white bread flour, plus extra for dusting

50g caster sugar, plus extra for coating

1 tsp fine salt

90ml whole milk

90ml water

7g/1½ tsp fast-action dried yeast

2 egg yolks

60g soured cream

1 tsp vanilla bean paste

50g unsalted butter, softened

1–2 litres sunflower oil, for deep-frying, plus extra for oiling

Measure the flour, sugar and salt into the bowl of a stand mixer and stir together really well.

Warm the milk and measured water to 25°C, or until it feels very slightly warm to the touch. Stir in the yeast and set aside for 5 minutes.

Pour this yeast mixture onto the flour mixture, then add the egg yolks, soured cream and vanilla bean paste. Stir well, then mix on a medium speed with the dough hook attachment for 5 minutes, until a dough forms. Turn the machine off and leave for 5 minutes.

Add the softened butter and mix on a medium-low speed until the butter is incorporated into the dough. Turn the machine speed up to medium and mix for 10–15 minutes, until the dough is smooth and well developed.

Lightly oil a large bowl. Shape the dough into a smooth ball and place in the bowl to prove at room temperature. This can take 2–4 hours.

When the dough has nearly doubled in size and looks puffy, scoop it out onto a work surface lightly dusted with flour and roll it out gently to a 2.5cm (1in) thickness.

Cut out 10 discs of dough with a 10cm (4in) cutter, then use a smaller 4cm (1½in) cutter to stamp out a hole from the middle of each disc (keep the holes and fry them for snacks, obviously).

Place the rings on a lightly oiled tray, cover loosely with clingfilm or a tea towel and leave to prove again, this time for 20–25 minutes.

When you are ready to fry the batter, heat a sturdy pan of oil to 160°C. Make sure the oil comes only one-third of the way up the sides of the pan, don't ever leave it alone and always use an oil thermometer to monitor the temperature.

Cut squares of kitchen paper, place on a tray and have them ready to rest each ring on as it comes out of the pan.

Gently drop the doughnuts into the oil in batches of 2–3 and fry for 2½ minutes on each side until golden. Remove with a slotted spoon and place on the kitchen paper squares to blot off the excess oil.

Leave to cool for 10 minutes, before dipping into caster sugar, before eating.

Gulab Jamun

In my last book, I mentioned that my mum makes gulab jamun once every five years and a couple of you wrote to me asking for the recipe. So I asked mum to write it down (for the first time) so you can make them yourself.

For those who don't know, they are delicate, soft, buttery, milk powder-based dumplings that are lightly fried before being simmered in lightly spiced sugar syrup. These are best served warm and only by the single one – only ever one – because they are very rich!

My mum works at light speed and never weighs anything, so during the testing of these I often had to run around behind her with scales and a cup. Biji, my grandma, in typical fashion kept interrupting and telling my mum where she was going wrong (she loves doing this). The sacrifice of a few arguments later (for your sakes) and we arrived at a really good batch of gulab jamun.

Makes 25

For the syrup

200g granulated sugar or caster
 sugar
500ml water
a few strands of saffron
3 cardamom pods, lightly crushed

For the dumplings

40g self-raising flour
150g milk powder
1 tsp ghee
100ml whole milk
40g fine semolina
250ml vegetable oil, or other
 neutral oil, for shallow-frying

Start with the syrup. Put the sugar in a large saucepan with the measured water, saffron and crushed cardamom. Set over a medium heat until the sugar has completely melted (you can stir it if you like).

We are aiming to take the syrup to a thread stage. What that means is, if you put some of the syrup into a bowl, let it cool a bit and then dip your index finger in, it should form a thread between your index finger and thumb when you touch them together. We look for this thread stage (110–112°C) because it shows us that the gulab jamun will absorb the syrup nicely; if the syrup is too thin, they will collapse and disintegrate. When it has reached this stage, remove from the heat.

For the dumplings, in a large bowl, stir together the self-raising flour and milk powder. Add the ghee and stir it through; it's not a lot, and it's important that you don't add more ghee because, if you do, the result will be too dense.

Warm the milk to body temperature (approx. 37°C) in a saucepan. Turn off the heat, then stir in the semolina. Let it sit for a few minutes before adding to the flour bowl and mixing to form a dough.

Now knead the dough for 10–15 minutes in the bowl, or by tipping it out onto a work surface if you find that easier.

Shape the dough into small balls by rolling pieces between your hands. My mum doesn't weigh them, but I did, and each ball was 8–11g.

Heat a sturdy saucepan of oil; we will be shallow-frying these gently, so the oil should only reach 140°C. Fry the balls in three batches, as you don't want to overcrowd the pan too much. When they go in to fry, the oil temperature will drop to about 125°C.

Fry low and slow for 10–15 minutes, turning them gently as you go. When they become a deep golden colour all around, they are ready. It's important not to rush this stage, or the centres will be raw. Drain on kitchen paper and repeat with the remaining dough balls.

Allow the dumplings to cool before adding to the syrup. The dough balls mustn't be hot and the syrup should be warm, but not hot. Add the dough balls to the syrup and cover the pan with a lid. Overnight they will absorb some of the syrup and expand slightly, so make sure you allow for this. If they're too big for the pan, transfer to a larger dish, making sure the dough balls are submerged and have enough room to grow.

The next day, place them in the fridge. They will keep in there for 3–4 days.

You can eat them cold or, as I like to, take one and warm it gently with a bit of the syrup in a small saucepan or in the microwave for 30 seconds.

Fried Pillows

I've made a lot of brioche doughnuts during my career; they are a lot richer than the regular variety. While testing the recipes for this book – and the brioche cubes especially – I would often fry off scraps of dough. I did it quite a lot and anyone who was in the kitchen at the time went a bit mad for them. The brioche develops a lovely golden crust while remaining super-fluffy inside. Please do give it a go; it's even worth making brioche dough for this specific purpose.

Makes 16

1 quantity Brioche dough (see page 76)
plain flour, for dusting
neutral oil, for deep-frying
caster sugar, for dipping
1 quantity Malt Chocolate Ganache (see page 26), for dipping (optional)

Get to the point in the brioche recipe when you have proved the dough in the fridge overnight (see page 76).

On a work surface lightly dusted with flour, roll the dough out to 5mm (¼in) thick, roughly 20cm (8in) square, and cut it into 16 smaller squares. Don't worry about being too precise here, as we are throwing them into the fryer.

Place the squares on a tray lined with baking paper, cover loosely with clingfilm and leave them to prove until poofy and fluffy. This should take 25–30 minutes.

Heat a sturdy pan of oil for frying to 160°C. Make sure the oil comes only one-third of the way up the sides of the pan, don't ever leave it alone and always use an oil thermometer to monitor the temperature.

Fry each brioche square for 3–4 minutes on each side, then remove from the pan with a slotted spoon and drain on a plate lined with kitchen paper. Dip the fried pillows in a shallow dish of the sugar and enjoy them warm, with your eyes closed. Dip them in the ganache, if you want to really push them over the edge.

Ricotta Bombolini

I think these are so perfect and fabulous, and absolutely brilliant when you need to throw together a quick dessert. When I worked at Llewelyn's in Herne Hill, I would often chuck these on the menu as a back-up if I knew I would sell out of some of the other desserts. In the end, people loved them so much that I had to start putting them on more often. They are like eating little pockets of sweet, fluffy air.

Serves 4

240g ricotta
2 eggs
40g caster sugar, plus extra to serve
110g plain flour
2 tsp baking powder
large pinch of fine salt
finely grated zest of 1 orange
neutral oil, for deep-frying

Strain the ricotta in a sieve over a bowl for 10 minutes, until the excess liquid has drained out. You should have 220g strained ricotta.

Whisk the eggs in a bowl, then whisk in the sugar to combine.

In a separate bowl, stir together the flour, baking powder and salt, then stir this into the whisked egg mixture. Grate in the orange zest. Finally, stir in the strained ricotta. Cover the bowl with clingfilm or a tea towel and let the mixture stand for 30 minutes.

When you are ready to fry the batter, heat a sturdy pan of oil to 160°C. Make sure the oil comes only one-third of the way up the sides of the pan, don't ever leave it alone and always use an oil thermometer to monitor the temperature.

Drop small tablespoons of batter into the oil and fry for 2 minutes on each side. These bombolini should naturally start to flip over by themselves after around 2 minutes. If not, gently encourage them over with a slotted spoon.

When they are evenly golden, remove from the oil to a plate lined with kitchen paper to soak up any excess.

Roll in caster sugar and enjoy warm.

Banana Fritters

This is a really light batter and a fantastic way to make a quick, impressive dessert for sharing. The batter can be used for other fritter-style desserts: think elderflower buds as fritti décor on a plate, or apple fritters served with an almond praline sauce. I tested this recipe a few times and decided that small baby bananas work best: they not only taste sweeter, but they also look cute.

Serves 4

For the fritters

1 tsp baking powder
10g/2 tsp cornflour
100g plain flour
pinch of fine salt
1 tbsp caster sugar, plus 50g for coating
110ml cold sparkling water
1 tbsp neutral oil, plus extra for deep-frying
6–7 small bananas, or other fruit of your choice
5g/1 tsp ground cinnamon

For the quick toffee sauce

75g unsalted butter
80g dark brown sugar
150g double cream
pinch of sea salt flakes

In a large bowl, thoroughly whisk together the baking powder, cornflour, plain flour, salt and 1 tbsp sugar. Gradually pour in the sparkling water, whisking to form a smooth batter. Finally, whisk in the 1 tbsp oil. Rest the batter in the fridge for 30 minutes.

Put all the ingredients for the toffee sauce – except the salt – into a saucepan and heat gently. When everything has melted and is simmering together, remove the pan from the heat and whisk everything together with the salt.

Meanwhile, heat a sturdy pan of oil, enough for deep-frying, to 180°C, or until a cube of bread browns in 30 seconds, taking all the usual precautions (see opposite).

Slice the bananas in half lengthways, or, if using larger bananas, slice in half and then in half again.

Dip the banana pieces in the batter to fully coat. Gently lower into the hot oil in small batches and stand back while they fry, turning them over every now and then to get an even colour. Fry for 5–8 minutes until wonderfully golden brown.

Drain on kitchen paper.

Stir the 50g caster sugar and the cinnamon together, then dip the banana fritters in the cinnamon sugar.

Eat immediately and serve with the toffee sauce.

Fruit Pies

I have made a lot of deep-fried fruit pies in my time. In most restaurants I would use puff pastry, as I had the space and time built into my schedule to factor in puff pastry production. I'm very much aware that a lot of you might not want to make puff pastry for the purpose of deep-frying it! So I've simplified the deep-fried fruit pie here for you. We are riffing on a rough puff pastry method here and sticking with strong flour which will help to deal with the amount of fat in the recipe and help the pastry to hold itself together while being filled, dipped in batter and deep-fried. You can switch up the fruit, I like using cherries (as we did here) when they are in season and, truth be told, I've even used pre-rolled puff pastry before when I'm being super lazy – which is not often but it does happen…

Makes 8

For the pastry
200g strong white bread flour, plus extra for dusting

10g/2 tsp caster sugar

3g/½ tsp fine salt

150g unsalted butter, chilled and cubed

50ml ice-cold water

For the apple filling
340g Bramley apples, peeled, cored and cut into 2cm (¾in) chunks

120g caster sugar

¼ tsp ground cinnamon

To finish
neutral oil, for deep-frying

1 quantity Banana Fritters batter (see page 105)

1 tsp ground cinnamon (optional)

100g caster sugar (optional)

icing sugar, for dusting (optional)

For the pastry, in a large bowl, combine the flour, sugar and salt and stir well.

Add the butter and either using your fingers, a food processor or a stand mixer with the paddle attachment, mix to the texture of crumbs; you aren't looking for fine crumbs here, they should be quite large. Add the ice-cold water and mix again to form a dough.

Very lightly flour a work surface. Tip the dough out onto the work surface and roll it out quickly lengthways to 5mm (¼in) thick. You don't need to be too precise here. Make a single 'turn', by folding the dough into thirds, like a letter. Place on a tray and refrigerate for 2 hours.

Turn the dough 90°, then repeat the folding and rolling to make another single turn.

Wrap tightly in clingfilm and refrigerate for 3–4 hours.

Meanwhile, place the prepared apples in a saucepan, add the sugar and stir well. Add 2 splashes of water and the cinnamon. Cook over a low heat for 10 minutes, stirring frequently, until the apples turn translucent. Transfer to a heatproof bowl and set aside to cool before placing in the fridge.

Fruit Pies

When you're ready to construct the pies, dust a work surface lightly with flour and roll the pastry out to roughly 32.5 x 28cm (13 x 11in). Fold in half lengthways to make a crease in the middle, then unfold. Use this crease as a guide to cut the pastry in half, giving you two strips.

Cut each strip across into four equal pieces. Each of these pieces will make a pie.

Take a piece of pastry and dollop 1 tablespoon of fruit filling in the middle to one side. Brush water around the edges of the pastry and fold the other half over. Seal the edges together by crimping with a fork. Repeat for the remaining pastry pieces and fruit filling.

Place the pies on a baking tray lined with baking paper and freeze.

Pour enough oil to deep-fry the pies into a large, deep saucepan and heat to 160°C, taking all the usual precautions (see page 104).

Dip the frozen pies into the batter on both sides and slowly lower into the hot oil, two at a time.

Fry for 4–5 minutes on each side until golden. Remove from the oil with a slotted spoon before draining the excess oil on kitchen paper.

Either mix the cinnamon and caster sugar together and dip the pies in it to serve, or simply dredge them in icing sugar.

Spicy Potato, Chilli and Cheese Choux

Here we make a choux pastry, a key skill for any pastry chef. The difference here from a regular choux recipe is that we will be folding mashed potato into the paste before deep-frying it and serving with a coriander dipping sauce.

Also – before you sugar fiends start complaining – I know this is a savoury recipe. *I know.* But, truly, they are so addictive that you might as well make a batch while preparing some of the sweet treats from this chapter, just while the fryer is on.

Makes 20–25

For the choux

1 large potato

olive oil

2g/½ tsp fine salt, plus 1 pinch

100ml water

100ml whole milk

100g unsalted butter

4g/scant 1 tsp caster sugar

100g strong white bread flour

120g whole eggs, lightly beaten

100g grated mature Cheddar cheese

1 large red chilli, finely chopped

2 spring onions, finely chopped

¼ tsp smoked paprika

freshly ground black pepper

neutral oil, for deep-frying

For the dipping sauce

bunch of coriander, both stalks and leaves

finely grated zest and juice of ½ unwaxed lemon

1 green chilli

½ tsp ground cumin

Preheat the oven to 180°C fan/200°C/gas mark 6.

Take the large potato and pierce the skin a few times with a knife, then rub with olive oil and sprinkle over the pinch of salt.

Bake in the oven until the middle is tender and soft (1–1½ hours, depending on size). Take out of the oven and allow to cool completely before scooping out the flesh, mashing it and keeping it aside. Feel free to crisp up the skin in the oven and eat it!

Heat the measured water, milk and butter with the sugar and the 2g/½ tsp salt in a saucepan over a medium heat. Take this to a rolling boil (where all the liquid is bubbling together).

Tip in the flour and stir constantly until the mixture comes away from the sides of the pan and forms a ball. Tip this out into a bowl and allow to cool slightly.

Beat the choux pastry gently to loosen it slightly. Add the eggs slowly and beat until the mixture is glossy. (It's important not to add too much egg here, as the potato will also loosen the mixture.) Fold in the potato, cheese, chilli, spring onions, paprika and black pepper.

Meanwhile, heat the oil in a large sturdy saucepan to 160°C, taking all the usual precautions (see page 104).

Drop small tablespoons of the choux into the hot oil and fry for a few minutes on each side. Remove and drain on kitchen paper.

For the dipping sauce, blend the coriander with the lemon zest and juice, green chilli, cumin, some salt and pepper and a splash of olive oil to form a paste. Loosen gently with a touch more oil and taste for seasoning.

Enjoy the choux warm with the dipping sauce and take a break from the sugar!

Tarts
Pies
Tarts
Pies

Not everything can be perfect.

As much as my parents didn't enjoy my career choice initially, the way I work and how I've got to where I am now is a direct result of them.

My mum – Jaz – is loud, as tough as an old boot, with a massive heart. She really loves tarte au citron – the one from M&S specifically – but never pronounces it properly. She's also a big fan of the cherry lemon pie in this chapter.

My dad is quiet and very practical. He's more into an almond-based tart and loves whisky, so the smoked almond and quince tart here is right up his street.

A lot of people expect me to say that I picked up my love of baking and pastry from my mum, but that's not true. What I did pick up from her was a level of resilience and an attitude of 'just getting on with it', whether that was intentional or not. Oh, and a strong cleaning game, she loves it.

My mum was born in Kenya. After her dad died when she was 14, she, along with her brother and mother – my Biji – packed their bags and moved to the UK. Mum says some of the first things she saw on their drive from the airport were market stalls and people wearing bell-bottoms. They moved here with no plan and no fixed place to live. Instead, they stayed with a cousin before moving into a bedsit for three years.

Biji couldn't speak any English (and still doesn't) and started work in a sewing factory, while my mum went to school on weekdays and worked with her on weekends, cutting stray threads off finished garments. During the week, my mum took care of the house by doing all the washing, cooking and cleaning. Her brother would go to college in the day and then to work in the evenings. My parents got married to each other when they were 30.

If you've read my first book, you'll know that I spent the first few years of my life living above a corner shop that my dad owned. Maybe it was that easy access to sweets and chocolate that cemented my deep love for – and career in making – desserts and pastry. We up and left when competition got tough for a convenience store as big supermarkets started opening up nearby. We packed our bags and went to live in Leyton, just off Francis Road.

My dad worked briefly as a security guard at Southwark Bridge for a newspaper company and my mum as a 'midday assistant' at mine and my brother's first primary school, Dawlish. My dad then started working for his brother's clothing company and would drive to Hertfordshire and back every day to do so.

I've always thought he's well clever, like very good at maths, always has been, despite only qualifying formally as an accountant in his forties when we had moved – yet again – to a charming place called Clayhall. He also taught karate in his late fifties. My mum rarely has time to dwell and instead her advice (more often than not, terribly received by me) is always to just shut up and get on with it.

The two of them definitely wanted *more* for me, I had the advantage of being schooled here AND going to university and then being offered the idea of a PhD…

Despite this, I waltzed blind into kitchens, with zero connections or idea of what I was doing or where I was going. I looked at my friends in grad schemes, and at my starting salary of £17k that never really increased, and I felt like I had failed. Really and truly, I stuck it out initially only because I wanted to prove a point to those who doubted me, my parents included. I really loved learning and all things food, but the environment was mostly about resilience and hard work. I spent my first few years working as a chef getting knocked back again and again. I take some responsibility for that, I was a bit rubbish and I'd get told off sometimes.

I understood that my basic salary wasn't going to increase dramatically on its own, so I started to take charge of that. I signed up to a chef agency and took private jobs at any possible opportunity, usually for corporate clients or in rich people's houses. I started making celebration cakes on the side, too. I set myself additional income goals and started hitting them. Yes, I wasn't sleeping much, but at least I felt like I wasn't swimming in custard any more. I was getting somewhere. I didn't have time for a relationship, but I made time to make money. That included working a double shift, going to a 24-hour supermarket to buy ingredients, baking a cake for a client into the early hours, then dropping it off before going back into work the next morning… It meant working an early shift before getting a food delivery sent to another client's house, then rushing off and cooking for a dinner party for 12, cleaning up and heading home before work again early the next morning.

Sure, some things don't go to plan, and not everything can be perfect, but at least you're trying. My parents, although they may not see it, are definitely big factors in my drive to work hard. While researching their backgrounds for this book, I got to hear so many stories of times when they may not have had much but still made it work. I'm so grateful that, because of their hard work, I'm able to do a job that I love and adore. It's very much because of them.

As I've said, I'm a big believer in trying, failing and getting right back up again after falling over. Building up resilience by making mistakes and learning from them. It's the same with pastry, isn't it? Too many people talk about how scary it is. It isn't. Sure, the first few times might be tricky, but don't let that put you off. Dust yourself off and just try again. And if you still can't roll out pastry, just grate it. **NO ONE REALLY MINDS.**

Cherry Lemon Pie

Years ago I went on holiday to Italy and, at the airport while waiting for my flight home, I grabbed a tart from one of the coffee shops. It looked like a mince pie, completely enclosed. I vividly remember the buttery pastry and the hit of the cherry, lemon and almond flavours. It was wonderful. Ever since, I have been asking my Italian mates about this airport tart, wondering if they have any idea what it is called. To this day I haven't quite figured it out. The closest I have come is *pasticciotto leccese* from Puglia, a custard tart filled with pastry cream. I've gone about recreating it instead with a baked lemon curd and cherries. The pastry is delicate, but really worth trying. I urge you to give it a go.

Makes a 20cm (8in) pie with a 2.5cm (1in) rim

For the pastry

150g unsalted butter, softened

75g caster sugar

finely grated zest of 1 unwaxed lemon

½ tsp almond extract

200g plain flour

¼ tsp baking powder

¼ tsp fine salt

2 egg yolks

For the filling

200g caster sugar, plus 15g/1 tbsp

juice of 4 lemons

65g unsalted butter

3 eggs, plus 1 egg for egg-washing

25g cornflour

100g amaretto-soaked cherries from a jar

10g/2 tsp demerara sugar

To make the pastry, beat the butter and sugar together with the lemon zest and almond extract.

In a separate bowl, stir the dry ingredients together well.

Add the egg yolks to the butter mixture and beat until fully combined, then tip in the dry ingredients and mix until a sticky dough forms.

Scrape the mixture out onto a flat tray lined with a large piece of baking paper or clingfilm. Fold over the top to seal and pat down to make a flattish disc. Chill in the fridge for at least 4 hours or until completely cold.

The dough will have set quite firmly in the fridge, so knead it through before rolling it out between 2 sheets of baking paper, working quickly, until it is 4–5mm (¼in) thick. If it starts to break or get too warm, simply chill before trying again.

Gently lower the pastry into a 20cm (8in) tart tin, pressing into the edges and leaving some overhang. Trim off the excess and set the scraps aside to use for the lid. Refrigerate for at least 30 minutes. Take the leftover pastry scraps and gently knead them together, then wrap tightly and chill in the fridge while you make the filling.

Cherry Lemon Pie

Now make the lemon curd. In a saucepan, heat the 200g of sugar with the lemon juice and butter. Whisk over a medium heat until the butter has melted.

In a separate bowl, whisk the 3 eggs together. Stir together the cornflour and the 15g/1 tbsp sugar and add this to the eggs, whisking well.

Pour the hot lemon mixture over the eggs while whisking, then return the mixture to the pan and stir continuously with a whisk until thickened and bubbling. Transfer to a heatproof container, leave to cool slightly and then chill in the fridge until cold.

Fill the tart case with the lemon curd and top with the cherries, pushing them in slightly. Chill again while you prepare the pie lid.

Roll the chilled pastry scraps out – again between sheets of baking paper – to a circle 4–5mm (¼in) thick, and place on top of the filled pie. Use the pastry overhang to seal the top by using your fingertips to push the two edges together all the way around. Don't worry too much about this, it should look a bit rustic. Chill again for 15 minutes.

Preheat the oven to 180°C fan/200°C/gas mark 6. Place a heavy, flat baking tray in the oven to heat up.

Take the chilled pie, egg-wash the top and sprinkle with demerara sugar.

Bake for 40–45 minutes; it should be golden on top.

Allow to cool completely before removing from the tin, otherwise it will break. Serve at room temperature.

Chocolate, Peanut and Damson Tart

This tart is *rich* and decadent. The chocolate peanut pastry is addictive and precious on its own. You could even roll it out and bake it as biscuits, or crumble it after baking for use as a crunchy garnish with a dessert, or use it as part of an entremet (see pages 138–171). It's unbelievably short. If you're not down with peanuts, you can substitute them for almonds or hazelnuts; the same goes for the peanut butter, an alternative nut butter will work just as well here.

Makes a 20cm (8in) tart

For the short chocolate and peanut pastry

60g caster sugar

15g/1 tbsp cocoa powder, plus extra for dusting

¼ tsp bicarbonate of soda

70g plain flour, plus extra for dusting

30g roasted, salted peanuts, well crushed (these will be part of the dough so don't leave any large pieces)

80g unsalted butter, chilled and cubed

1 egg yolk

For the baked chocolate filling

3 eggs

110g caster sugar

100g dark chocolate, chopped

70g milk chocolate, chopped

11g/scant 1 tbsp unsalted butter

120g double cream

2g/large pinch of sea salt flakes

100g damson jam

80g peanut butter

Place all the dry ingredients for the pastry in the bowl of a stand mixer fitted with the paddle attachment. Add the crushed peanuts and butter and mix until fine crumbs form. Add the egg yolk and mix until a dough comes together.

Scoop into a piece of clingfilm, press flat and refrigerate for a minimum of 4 hours.

Roll out to 4mm (¼in) thick on a work surface dusted with flour.

Line a 20cm (8in) round pastry ring with the chocolate pastry by cutting out a circle for the base and strips for the sides. Refrigerate for 30 minutes until the pastry is cold again. Be careful when handling as this pastry is tricky to work with and very delicate.

Preheat the oven to 160°C fan/180°C/gas mark 4. Line the pastry case with baking paper, fill with baking beans and bake for 30 minutes.

Remove the baking beans and paper and return to the oven for a further 10 minutes.

For the filling, whisk the eggs and sugar together in a stand mixer until pale and thick.

Melt both the chocolates and the butter together (see page 41). Gently pour into the whisking eggs with the machine on a medium speed. Pour in the cream and mix to incorporate, then fold in the salt.

Preheat the oven to 150°C fan/170°C/gas mark 3½.

Spoon the jam into the tart case, then place in the freezer for 10 minutes. Spoon over the peanut butter in an even layer, then pour over the chocolate filling and bake the tart for 35 minutes.

Allow the tart to cool down fully before removing from the tin. If you like it slightly gooey, serve immediately. Alternatively put it in the fridge for 4 hours to fully set. Dust with cocoa before serving.

Quince and Smoked Almond Tart

I guarantee that 75 per cent of you won't make this. That's okay. For the 25 per cent wanting to take the risk, let's do it together. The flavour profile of this tart is really special, very unique: fruity, smoky, slightly acidic, buttery... like an aged whisky. We don't blind-bake the tart case here, as there's no need. The butter from the frangipane mingles with the raw dough and infuses it, just be sure to press the pastry thinly enough into the tin. Use smoked almonds with the skin on if you can find them, simply blitz them to a powder and brace yourself.

A NOTE: This will make more quince than you need, there's no point in poaching one or two quince, so keep any leftovers in the syrup and serve over pavlova or with yoghurt and granola for breakfast.

Makes a 23cm (9in) tart

For the quince

1.9 litres water

400g granulated sugar (or caster sugar)

½ lemon

4 quince

For the sweet pastry

175g plain flour

50g caster sugar

120g plus ½ tbsp unsalted butter, chilled and cubed

¼ tsp fine salt

1 egg yolk

For the smoked almond frangipane

100g unsalted butter

50g light brown sugar

50g caster sugar

2 eggs

60g smoked almonds, ground, plus a few extra, crushed, for the top

40g ground almonds

20g plain flour

Start by poaching the quince. Put the measured water and sugar in a large saucepan. Squeeze in the lemon half and add the husk to the pan. Peel the quince, throwing the skins into the saucepan, then cut the quince into quarters and add to the pan.

Make a cartouche from baking paper: cut a circle of paper to fit the saucepan, then run it under a tap to wet it before scrunching it up. Un-scrunch it and place on top of the quince in the pan, with a plate on top to hold everything down.

Set the pan over a medium heat. Once it comes to the boil, reduce the heat to a simmer and cook for 2–2½ hours, or until the quince are tender when a knife is inserted. Take off the heat and leave to sit for a few hours before pouring into a container and placing both quince and liquor in the fridge.

The quince will develop in colour over the next few days. When ready to use them, remove the cores and strain the skins from the poaching liquid. (Reduce the poaching liquid if drizzling over a dessert.)

Now for the pastry. Place all the ingredients except the egg yolk in the bowl of a stand mixer and mix with the paddle attachment until the butter is well incorporated and the mixture resemble fine crumbs. Add the yolk and mix until a crumble forms.

Reserve a handful of crumble, then press the rest into a 23cm (9in) tart tin, making the base thin enough that you can almost see the tin through it, but being more generous with the thickness of the sides. Place in the freezer while you make the frangipane.

Clarify the butter. To do this, gently warm the butter in a saucepan until melted; the milk proteins will rise to the top and start to bubble. Keep heating gently until the top clears. Pour through a muslin or fine cloth into a heatproof bowl and leave to cool fully. Place in the fridge to firm up.

Beat the cooled clarified butter and sugars together until glossy and homogeneous, then add the eggs and beat in.

Add both types of ground almonds and the flour, mixing well.

Preheat the oven to 180°C fan/200°C/gas mark 6 and place a heavy baking tray inside to heat up.

Remove the cold pastry case from the freezer, spoon in the frangipane to form an even layer, then cut each quince quarter in half and arrange in the tin (use enough to just cover the frangipane).

Scatter over the reserved handful of crumble mix and a few crushed smoked almonds.

Place the tart directly on the hot baking tray and bake for 50–60 minutes until golden on top.

Serve warm, with some of the quince poaching liquor drizzled over the top and a dollop of crème fraîche. Or, for those with a sweeter tooth, serve with crème anglaise.

Roasted Delica Pumpkin, Feta and Rye Galette

Pumpkin *is* sort of sweet and, if you can get your hands on it, Delica pumpkin is my absolute favourite. This is a beautiful way to make a galette, adding rye flour to a rough puff gives it a twist and complements the puréed pumpkin nicely.

Makes a 25cm (10in) galette

For the pastry

150g unsalted butter, frozen and then grated

160g strong white bread flour, plus extra for dusting

40g wholemeal rye flour

1 tsp sea salt flakes

50ml ice-cold water

For the pumpkin filling

1 Delica pumpkin, or other dense-fleshed pumpkin (mine was 1.15kg), deseeded

1 large red chilli, halved

3 medium shallots, peeled and halved

4–5 large garlic cloves, skins on

extra virgin olive oil

a few thyme sprigs

sea salt flakes and freshly ground black pepper

To serve

olive oil

sage leaves

feta cheese

1 large red chilli, sliced, mixed with 4 tbsp Moscatel vinegar

Re-freeze the grated butter for 10 minutes.

Place both the flours and the salt in the bowl of a stand mixer with the paddle attachment, or in a large bowl if using your hands, and mix well. Add the grated frozen butter and mix with the flours until it is fully coated. Add the measured water and mix until a loose dough forms.

Tip the dough onto a work surface and bring it together quickly. Flour the work surface lightly and then roll the dough quickly to the length of an A4 sheet of paper, then fold into thirds. Rotate by 90° and repeat.

Wrap in baking paper or clingfilm and refrigerate for 2 hours.

Meanwhile, preheat the oven to 180°C fan/200°C/gas mark 6. Cut the pumpkin into slices around 2.5cm (1in) thick and arrange on a baking tray lined with baking paper, along with the halved chilli and shallots.

Wrap the garlic cloves in a piece of foil (drizzle with olive oil before you seal the foil package). Put this on the tray with the pumpkin.

Drizzle over 5–6 tablespoons of olive oil, add a liberal sprinkling of salt and pepper and the thyme.

Bake for 30 minutes, or until the pumpkin is tender, then remove from the oven and allow to cool. Squeeze the garlic from its skin. Remove the skin from half the pumpkin and blitz in a food processor with the garlic, roasted chilli and 1 tablespoon of olive oil to form a paste. (Reserve the shallots.)

Preheat the oven to 180°C fan/200°C/gas mark 6.

Roll the pastry out on a lightly floured work surface to a circle about 32.5cm (13in) in diameter, 2mm (⅛in) thick. Place this disc on a large baking tray lined with baking paper. Spread the pumpkin paste on the pastry, leaving a 1cm (½in) border around the edge.

Arrange the roasted pumpkin pieces on top, then fold the pastry around the edge over onto itself. Drizzle with olive oil and bake for 35 minutes.

Meanwhile, make the crispy sage leaves. Take a small saucepan and pour in enough olive oil to reach a depth of 1cm (½in). Warm the oil gently. Drop in a few sage leaves at a time and fry for a few seconds until they shrivel slightly and become crisp. Drain on kitchen paper.

Remove the tart from the oven, top with the roasted shallot segments and crispy sage, crumble over the feta and finally top with the sliced red chilli in vinegar.

Enjoy warm or cold.

Peach, Raspberry and Apple Cobbler

I think everyone should have a staple cobbler recipe. A cobbler is like a cross between a cake batter and a biscuit or scone dough, though where it lands on that spectrum depends, I guess, on who's making it. I love the versatility that comes with a cobbler. You can keep the topping and switch out the fruit for whatever is best in season and available to you. My tip is always to taste the fruit first; you might want to reduce the sugar if it's naturally very sweet, or up it if the fruit is particularly sour.

Serves 6–8

For the filling

1 large Bramley apple, about 225g

360g peaches

150g raspberries

115g caster sugar

juice of ½ lemon

For the topping

150g plain flour

1 tsp baking powder

pinch of fine salt

95g caster sugar

95g unsalted butter, chilled and cubed

30ml milk

Preheat the oven to 180°C fan/200°C/gas mark 6.

Peel the apple, remove the core and chop into large chunks. Stone the peaches and cut them into equal-size pieces. Mix both fruits with the raspberries in a ceramic ovenproof dish, measuring about 25 x 18 x 5cm (10 x 7 x 2in).

Add the sugar and lemon juice and mix really well with the fruit.

Make the topping by stirring together the flour, baking powder, salt and sugar in a large bowl. Add the cold cubed butter and mix until you reach fine crumb stage. Add the milk to bring it together into a soft, thick batter (don't mix this for too long, just until it comes together).

Dollop large tablespoons of batter over the top of the fruit in the dish. There's no need to completely cover it; the beauty of a cobbler is seeing the fruit bubble over the topping.

Bake for 35–40 minutes, until the topping is golden and the fruit is bubbling. Test that the cobbler topping is fully baked by gently lifting a bit up with a spoon: if it looks like raw cake batter inside or underneath, return it to the oven for a further 10–15 minutes.

Serve warm with ice cream, custard or cream. You know the drill.

Apple and Rosemary Tarte Tatin

This a particularly glorious tarte tatin; the difference from the norm being that here we are making a quick rough puff and a caramel spiked with rosemary and bay. The result is a wonderfully dark, sweet-and-sour apple topping with a crisp, buttery pastry underneath that stays crisp for a while, even after being drenched in custard or melted ice cream.

I use strong white flour here, which I mostly always use for puff pastry, as it needs a bit more strength than plain flour can provide, due to all the fat and layers that we will be building within it.

Makes a 20cm (8in) tarte tatin

For the pastry

200g strong white bread flour,
   plus extra for dusting

½ tsp fine salt

185g unsalted butter, frozen

60ml ice-cold water

10ml/2 tsp white wine vinegar

For the filling

6 Bramley or Cox apples

200g caster sugar

30g unsalted butter

2–3 rosemary sprigs

1–2 bay leaves

To make the pastry, in the bowl of a stand mixer fitted with the paddle attachment, stir together the flour and salt. Grate in the frozen butter. Mix until mixed through; we want it to stay lumpy with visible bits of butter, so this is just to coat the butter in flour.

Stir together the measured water and vinegar, then add it to the bowl and mix until a dough forms.

Scoop the pastry out onto a sheet of baking paper, lay another piece on top and roll it out lengthways. Remove the paper, then fold the pastry into three like a letter (this is called a single turn). Place in the fridge for 2 hours, then roll out again and complete another single turn, turn the pastry by 90° and fold again. Place in the fridge for another 2 hours, then complete another 2 single turns and chill for a final 2 hours.

Roll out one 25cm (10in), 5mm (¼in) thick circle of pastry on a work surface dusted with flour and chill. Gather any scraps together and wrap tightly in clingfilm for use in something else!

Preheat the oven to 180°C fan/200°C/gas mark 6.

Prep the apples by peeling them and halving. Remove the cores.

Take your tatin pan (or ovenproof frying pan) and set it over a medium heat. Sprinkle the sugar in and gently melt until caramelized to an amber colour. Add the butter and stir well to melt and mix with the caramel, then add the rosemary sprigs and bay leaves and remove from the heat. Place the apples in the pan, core-sides down.

Place the disc of pastry on top of the apples, gently tucking the edges over the sides of the apples (be careful not to burn your hands). Place in the oven and bake for 30 minutes.

Reduce the oven temperature to 160°C fan/180°C/gas mark 4 and bake for a further 10 minutes.

Take out of the oven and let it sit for a few minutes. Carefully place a plate on top of the frying pan and, wearing oven gloves, flip it over before removing the pan.

Enjoy with ice cream, custard or cream (or all three, in true Jeremy Lee-style).

Mince Pies

I advise you to make a batch of mincemeat early in September
and seal it in a large container. Every few weeks, give it a stir and
add another glug of brandy, if needed. This is all part of the joy and
build-up to Christmas. Better still, make enough so you have some
for the next year, too. This recipe makes enough mincemeat to keep
you going throughout the Christmas period and beyond!

Most mince pies are made with either a buttery shortcrust pastry
or puff pastry, and this is a topic of dispute among many of my friends.
I've been making my mince pies with this cream cheese pastry for a
long time and I think it's the one (for me).

The amount of fat in this dough is what gives it the characteristic
flakiness that you get with puff pastry, without the work involved. It
doesn't puff up in the same way (that would be pure sorcery), instead
it stays light and crisp, treading the line between puff and shortcrust...

Makes 16 mince pies

For the mincemeat

1kg Bramley apples

350g unsalted butter, plus
    1 tbsp

1kg dark brown sugar

10g/2 tsp ground cinnamon

15g/1 tbsp ground allspice

7g/1½ tsp ground nutmeg

finely grated zest of 3 oranges
    and the juice of 2

finely grated zest of 2 unwaxed
    lemons and the juice of 1

1kg sultanas

1.5kg raisins

1kg currants

500g dried unsweetened
    cranberries

200ml brandy (or rum)

For the cream cheese pastry

250g plus 2 tbsp unsalted
    butter, plus extra for the tin

300g full-fat cream cheese, at
    room temperature

300g plain flour, plus extra for
    dusting

1 tsp fine salt

1½ tsp caster sugar

1 egg, lightly beaten

demerara sugar, for sprinkling

For the mincemeat, peel and core the apples and then chop them finely.

In a saucepan, melt the butter with the sugar. Add the ground spices and heat gently for around 10 minutes. Add the orange and lemon juices.

Place all the dried fruits, the apple and the zests in a large container, giving them a good stir. Pour in the sugar-butter mixture and carefully mix together well. Once mixed, add the brandy and stir well.

You can seal the mincemeat in airtight jars if you are keeping it for next year. Alternatively, if I'm making this in September for the coming Christmas, I pop it in a large clean container with an airtight lid, opening it every few weeks and adding a bit more brandy!

To make the pastry, beat the butter until soft, then add the cream cheese and mix together quickly.

Separately stir the flour, salt and sugar together, then add to the cream cheese mixture and beat in quickly until a sticky dough forms.

Scrape onto a sheet of baking paper or clingfilm and wrap tightly. Press into a flat disc and refrigerate overnight.

Roll the pastry out to a rough rectangle, 4mm (¼in) thick, on a lightly floured work surface. Place on a tray lined with baking paper and refrigerate for 20 minutes. Cut out eight 9cm (3½in) circles and eight 4cm (1½in) circles, re-rolling the trimmings if needed, and return to the fridge.

Liberally butter a muffin tin and chill in the fridge. Taking care to keep the pastry discs cold (the pastry gets soft quickly, so remove from the fridge one by one), thin out the edges of the larger discs a little and press into the holes of the cold muffin tin. The pastry should overhang the top of the holes by at least 5mm (¼in). Fill each hole up to the top with mincemeat.

Thin out the edges of the smaller discs and place on top of the mincemeat (the discs shouldn't completely reach the edges). Fold the overhang of the cases over the lids and chill for a further hour in the fridge.

Preheat the oven to 180°C fan/200°C/gas mark 6.

Egg-wash the tops of the pies and, using a sharp knife, pierce a small hole in the middle of each. Sprinkle with demerara sugar and bake for 30–35 minutes, until golden and the filling is oozing over the lids a bit.

Run a palette knife around the pies while still warm (be careful, the filling will be hot) and release from the tin. Enjoy with brandy butter, cream or ice cream.

Miso Caramel and Chocolate Tart with a Crunchy Cereal Base

Using a mix of cereal and melted chocolate for the base of a tart brings out my inner child. The base here is so madly addictive that it's quite hard to not eat it before pressing it into the tart case. (Perhaps it's better to make a double batch of the base so you can do just that.)

The use of a swirled-through miso caramel means that you don't need to sprinkle sea salt flakes on top. Unless you're my friend Terri, of course (see page 24).

Makes a 20cm (8in) tart

For the tart case

100g dark chocolate, chopped
40g unsalted butter, melted
30g roasted hazelnuts, lightly crushed
90g bran flakes cereal, lightly crushed
pinch of sea salt flakes

For the miso caramel

35g caster sugar
7g/½ tbsp unsalted butter
65ml double cream
1 tbsp white miso paste

For the dark chocolate ganache

200g double cream
60g milk chocolate, chopped
90g dark chocolate, chopped

Start with the tart case. Melt the chocolate and butter together over a bain-marie (see page 41) or in short bursts in the microwave.

In a large bowl, mix together the hazelnuts, bran flakes and salt. Pour in the melted chocolate mixture and stir well.

Press into a 20cm (8in) tart tin, into the bottom and up the sides. It doesn't matter if it doesn't reach to the very top of the tin, you want just enough to give you a good edge of roughly 2.5cm (1in) deep. Place in the fridge to chill for up to an hour.

For the miso caramel, make a direct caramel in a saucepan by placing it over a medium heat, sprinkling in the sugar and letting it melt to a dark caramel. Add the butter and whisk well, then pour in the cream and let it bubble for a minute.

Remove from the heat and whisk in the miso paste. Set aside for a few minutes. When the caramel has cooled slightly, pour it into a heatproof dish and allow to cool further. We want it to be at pouring consistency but not *hot*.

Miso Caramel and Chocolate Tart with a Crunchy Cereal Base

To make the ganache, in the same pan that you've just poured the caramel from, add the cream and heat until steaming.

Place both the chocolates into a large heatproof bowl and pour over the hot cream. Let it sit for a minute before stirring with a whisk from the middle outwards until melted and smooth. Pour into the chilled tart shell and let it sit for 2 minutes.

Take the miso caramel and drizzle thickly all over the ganache. Use a butter knife to drag the caramel through the ganache to form swirls, then place in the fridge to set for 4 hours.

This will keep in the fridge for 2–3 days, but is best eaten as soon as the ganache has set.

Kadaif Pie

If you're well versed in Middle Eastern food, you will have eaten
kunafa/kanafeh/künefe before. It's a delicious sweet cheese
dessert made using either kadaif pastry, shredded filo pastry or a
semolina-style dough. There are many iterations of this gorgeous
dessert depending on region, and I wanted to create a version of it
that you can assemble in advance, pop in the fridge and then
bake when guests come round. Really decadent and moreish, this
is best made in a dish with the hot syrup poured over after baking.
Typically I wouldn't suggest buying pastry, *but*, on this occasion, I
think it's a must for the sake of ease. You can find good-quality
kadaif in most Turkish supermarkets.

   Assembling and baking these tarts in a cast-iron frying pan works
very well, because it ensures that the base gets nice and golden.
But, if you don't have one, you can adjust the recipe to fit the
baking dish of your choice: just follow the method and up the
quantities to suit your dish, as it's a very flexible recipe.

Kadaif Pie

**Makes two 15cm (6in) pies
(each serves 2–3)**

For the pie

90g unsalted butter, melted, plus
 10g softened butter, for brushing

100g full-fat cream cheese, at
 room temperature

pinch of sea salt flakes

260g (2 balls) mozzarella

150g kadaif pastry

For the syrup

100g caster sugar

160ml water

2 tbsp good-quality dark honey

a few sprigs of thyme

1 tbsp orange blossom water

40g ground pistachios

Preheat the oven to 170°C fan/190°C/gas mark 5.

Brush two 15cm (6in) cast-iron frying pans – or other ovenproof dishes of your choice (see the recipe introduction) – liberally with the 10g softened butter.

In a large bowl, beat the cream cheese until soft and add the salt. Tear the mozzarella into large chunks and mix this through the cream cheese.

Take about half of the kadaif pastry (no need to be too strict with measurements here). Divide it between the frying pans or dishes and press down into the bases, trying to patch it up so there's not too many holes. Pull the pastry a little up the sides to stop the cheese mixture from leaking out; we want to enclose it.

Divide the cream cheese mixture between the pans or dishes.

Top with the remaining kadaif pastry, dividing it between the pans or dishes and pressing down gently to cover the cheese; you should compact the pastry slightly in doing so.

Either place these in the fridge ready for baking later the same day, or drizzle over the melted butter now, dividing it evenly between the 2 pies.

Bake for 35–40 minutes until golden and crispy on top.

Meanwhile, make the syrup by heating the sugar and measured water in a saucepan until dissolved. Bring to the boil for a few minutes. Add the honey off the heat with the thyme and orange blossom and stir well.

When the kadaif pies are cooked, take out of the oven and – while they are still hot – pour over the syrup evenly, dividing it between the two pies. Finish by sprinkling ground pistachios over the top and serve warm in the pans or dishes.

Entr
Entr
Entr
Entr

emet

emet

emet

emet

I like to think of my teaching style as less hand-holding, more cheerleading.

I think this is mainly because I spent far too long feeling bound by rules in pastry, fearing stepping outside of what I was taught and thinking very stringently, that I couldn't possibly chuck in a bit of something and switch out this for that. There's nothing wrong with that at the beginning, rules and guidelines are in place in certain areas for a reason; they help to ensure consistency! With time, I realized that I could make things my own and I developed more confidence in the kitchen. This helped me, not only to climb the ranks quickly, but to bake and cook a lot better. Something I really want to pass on to you is developing the confidence, freedom and creativity to step out of the rules to make things your own. The entremet chapter is the perfect space for this.

I have been gagging to include a deep dive into the world of entremets ever since writing my first book. An entremet by definition is a multi-layered, multi-textured dessert. Done correctly, it's a clever way of marrying together a good few flavours and textures. You can layer the components into a glass, or into a metal ring mould so they become a layer cake, or even set the different elements in silicone moulds, freezing then unmoulding inserts to be placed inside a mousse or ganache. The possibilities are vast and endless, so it was hard to whittle down key recipes for this chapter without writing an entire book on just entremet elements (an idea for the future perhaps?). Try not to feel daunted when you look at an example of a full entremet recipe in this chapter, instead read through the whole lot from start to finish before deciding if you want to take on the challenge.

And if you want to change one of the elements then go for it! Get creative and think about what flavours and textures work well together, and give it a try. And if you decide that actually you only want to make one of the elements on its own first, like the crème brûlée custard, which I highly recommend, then do that! Or you might fancy taking sourdough crumbs and running them through a parfait, or crumbling the offcuts of the highly addictive chocolate and peanut pastry and using them as a garnish. You see? Use this chapter to build up your confidence and have a play around with the recipes, it's all part of the **FUN.**

How to build an entremet

My ultimate goal in this chapter is to encourage you to get creative and push yourself to make creations of your own. To help you to do that, I have broken this chapter down into the following elements.

Over the next few pages you'll find recipes for each component part. All these recipes make a similar quantity, so it's easy for you to use this chapter as a pick and mix, taking an element from each section and creating something fun.

With the components here, you can choose to build one large entremet or create multiple miniatures. The important thing is to consider carefully how each component will fit together.

Give these a go and then jump into the other recipes later on in the chapter and pair a few different recipe components together to make creations of your own. This chapter is here to help you cut loose and experiment! Keep a notepad nearby and take note of your new creations.

① SHEET SPONGES (AND PASTRY)

These will form the base. An entremet can sit on a sponge base that's soaked in a syrup (or not), it can be enclosed in a tart case, or pastry can be baked flat like a biscuit and with an unmoulded mousse arranged prettily on top. You can take pastry recipes from the Tarts & Pies chapter in this book (see pages 110–137) and use them to make mini tart cases, or whatever else you fancy…

② SOAKING SYRUPS

Use these to add **MORE** flavour to a sheet sponge, and to moisten it. Be careful you don't go overboard with syrup, though, as that can lead to a disintegrated cake.

③ SPREADABLES

These are a good way to add sharpness and a contrasting texture to an entremet. A sauce can be housed inside as a hidden runny filling, or used to layer up sponge or biscuit layers.

④ MOUSSES OR FILLERS

Typically, this forms one of the main parts of an entremet. If using a mousse, it shouldn't be so heavy or dominant in flavour that it takes away from the other elements; it should, instead, complement them. Mousse works really well frozen into a silicone mould; you can also hide another pre-frozen element inside it. You could also set mousses or fillers in a glass, roll them into a roulade, or layer them up between sheets of sponge.

⑤ GLAZES OR GARNISHES

A glaze is optional, but it can help to round off the whole thing. Traditionally you glaze an entremet once it is frozen, as it coats better. An alternative is to top the entremet with a garnish.

⑥ CRUNCHY BITS

These can be folded through a smooth mousse or other filler to add texture, sprinkled on top of a sponge or biscuit, served alongside an entremet, or even on top of it.

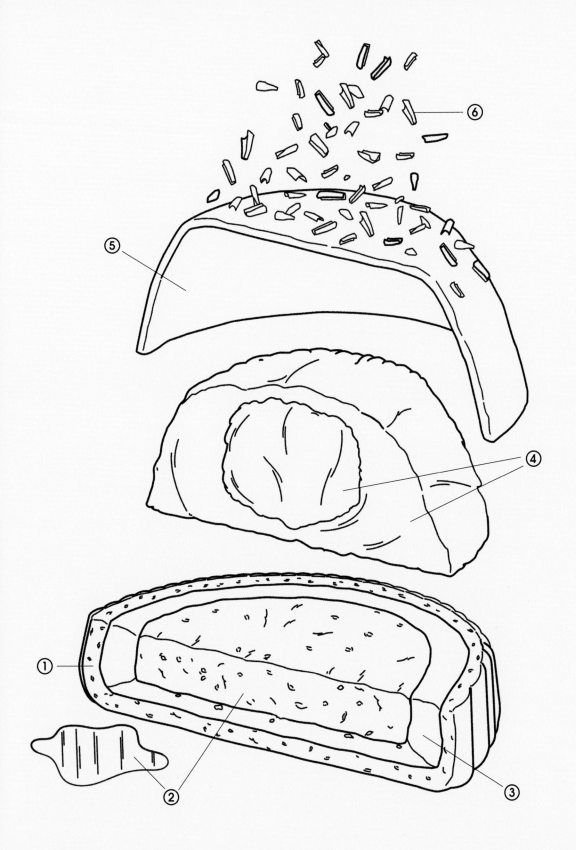

Sheet Sponges

For all these sponges, you need to prepare a baking tray, first by lightly buttering it and then by lining the base with baking paper. It helps to line it a little up the sides as well, as this will help you to release the sponge once baked.

Once removed from the oven, allow the sponge to cool on the tray for 10 minutes before placing a larger sheet of baking paper directly on top of the cake and flipping it over to release it. Pull off the layer of paper that the cake was baked upon and only use the cake once cooled.

These sheet sponges can be wrapped tightly in clingfilm on a flat baking tray and stored at room temperature for 2 days, or frozen for up to 30 days.

All the sheet sponges make about 500g cake batter, to fit a lipped baking tray measuring 38 x 25 x 2.5cm (15 x 10 x 1in) .

Almond Jaconde Sponge

100g ground almonds

100g icing sugar

30g plain flour

2g/scant ½ tsp fine salt

100g egg whites

15g/1 tbsp caster sugar

3 eggs

20g/1½ tbsp unsalted butter, melted, plus extra butter for the baking tray

Preheat the oven to 200°C fan/220°C/gas mark 7. Butter a baking tray and line it with baking paper.

Sift together the ground almonds, icing sugar, flour and salt into a large bowl.

In a separate bowl, whisk the egg whites until frothy, then add the caster sugar and whisk to soft peaks.

Whisk the 3 eggs into the bowl of dry ingredients until a loose paste forms.

Fold the whipped egg whites into the paste in three batches, while drizzling in the butter around the edges of the bowl.

Pour the batter into the prepared baking tray and smooth right to the edges with an offset palette knife. Gently tap the tray on a work surface to make sure the mixture is evenly spread.

Bake for 7 minutes, until golden and springy to the touch.

Roasted Peanut and Malt Sponge

unsalted butter, for the baking tray

65g icing sugar

45g roasted peanuts, blitzed

2g/scant ½ tsp fine salt

90g wholemeal spelt flour

50g/3½ tbsp malt powder

170g egg whites

80g caster sugar

Preheat the oven to 170°C fan/190°C/gas mark 5. Butter a baking tray and line it with baking paper.

Stir together the icing sugar, blitzed peanuts, salt, spelt flour and malt powder.

Make a French meringue by whisking the egg whites in a bowl until frothy, then slowly whisking in the caster sugar until soft peaks form.

Sift the dry ingredients over the meringue in three batches, gently folding them in each time. There will be some crushed larger pieces of peanut left in the sieve – this is a good thing – hold them back.

Pour onto the prepared baking tray and smooth with an offset palette knife right to the edges. Gently tap the tray on a work surface to make sure the mixture is evenly spread, then sprinkle the leftover peanuts from the sieve over the top.

Bake for 14 minutes, until golden and dry to the touch.

Short Chocolate and Peanut Pastry

Makes a 20cm (8in) tart case, or 8 small cases, as pictured on page 170

60g caster sugar

15g/1 tbsp cocoa powder, plus extra for dusting

¼ tsp bicarbonate of soda

70g plain flour, plus extra for dusting

30g roasted, salted peanuts, well crushed (these will be part of the dough so don't leave any large pieces)

80g unsalted butter, chilled and cubed

1 egg yolk

Place all the dry ingredients for the pastry in the bowl of a stand mixer fitted with the paddle attachment. Add the crushed peanuts and butter and mix until fine crumbs form. Add the egg yolk and mix until a dough comes together.

Scoop into a piece of clingfilm, press flat and refrigerate for a minimum of 4 hours.

Roll out to 4mm (¼in) thick on a work surface dusted with flour. Line the tart ring/s or tart case/s with the pastry.

Refrigerate for half an hour until the pastry is cold again.

Preheat the oven to 160°C fan/180°C/gas mark 4. Line the pastry cases with baking paper and baking beans and bake for 17 minutes, then remove the baking beans and paper and return to the oven for a further 10 minutes.

Allow to cool fully before using.

Mango and Lime Sponge

Makes a 25 x 12.5cm (10 x 5in) sponge
unsalted butter, for the
    baking tray
4 eggs
120g caster sugar
80g plain flour
4g/scant 1 tsp baking powder
2g/scant ½ tsp fine salt
90g mango purée
finely grated zest and juice of
    1 lime
10g/2 tsp neutral oil

———

Preheat the oven to 160°C fan/
180°C/gas mark 4. Line a 25 x
12.5cm (10 x 5in) baking tray with
baking paper.

Whisk the eggs and caster sugar to
ribbon stage (see page 20, Ras
Malai Cake) on a medium speed.

Separately stir together the plain
flour, baking powder and salt.

When the egg mixture has reached
ribbon stage, pour it into a large
bowl and fold in the mango purée,
lime zest and juice and oil.

Finally, sift over the dry ingredients
and fold together, making sure
there are no lumps of the flour
mixture.

Pour onto the prepared baking tray
and smooth with an offset palette
knife to the edges. Gently tap the
tray on a work surface to make
sure the mixture is evenly spread.

Bake for 18 minutes, until golden
and springy to the touch.

Crunchy Hazelnut Dacquoise

unsalted butter, for the
    baking tray
220g egg white
80g caster sugar
80g icing sugar
pinch of salt
120g roasted ground hazelnuts

———

Preheat the oven to 160°C fan/
180°C/gas mark 4. Butter a baking
tray and line it with baking paper.

Make a French meringue by
whisking the egg whites in a bowl,
then slowly whisking in the caster
sugar until soft peaks form.

In a separate bowl, stir together the
icing sugar, salt and hazelnuts.

In three batches, sift the dry
ingredients into the meringue and
gently fold them in. There will be
some hazelnut pieces left in the
sieve. Reserve them.

Pour onto the prepared baking tray
and smooth with an offset palette
knife to the edges. Gently tap the
tray on a work surface to make
sure the mixture is evenly spread,
then sprinkle the leftover hazelnuts
from the sieve over the top.

Bake for 15 minutes, then reduce
the oven temperature to 140°C
fan/160°C/gas mark 3 and cook
for a further 5 minutes, until dry to
the touch.

Light Flourless Chocolate Cake

unsalted butter, for the baking tray
5 eggs, separated
85g caster sugar, plus 95g
2g/scant ½ tsp fine salt
60g cocoa powder, sifted

———

Preheat the oven to 170°C fan/
190°C/gas mark 5. Butter a baking
tray and line it with baking paper.

Make a French meringue by whisking
the egg whites in a bowl until frothy,
then slowly whisking in the 85g of
sugar until soft peaks form.

Whisk the egg yolks in a separate
bowl with the 95g sugar until thick,
pale and at ribbon stage (see page
20, Ras Malai Cake), then whisk in
the salt.

Fold the two egg mixtures together
in three batches, alternating with
the sifted cocoa powder, to form
a smooth batter.

Pour onto the prepared baking tray
and smooth with an offset palette
knife right to the edges. Gently tap
the tray on a work surface to make
sure the mixture is evenly spread.

Bake for 20–22 minutes, until springy
to the touch and cooked through.

Soaking Syrups

A soaking syrup isn't always necessary in an entremet, but it can really help to dial up that flavour. Used correctly, it can also assist in keeping a sponge moist. When using a syrup with a sponge, it's important to remember that only one of the elements needs to be warm. We don't want to damage the crumb of the cake, nor do we want to drench it, making it too sweet to eat. The idea is that the syrup packs a punch; it will only be a small element of the finished entremet, which is why it's important that it's flavourful.

To make a sugar syrup, all you need to do is warm sugar in a saucepan with a liquid until dissolved. If adding another ingredient, such as an alcohol, do so only once the syrup is off the heat. If infusing a warm syrup with other ingredients, strain it before use. You can make any of the following recipes in bigger batches and store in the fridge in an airtight container, where they will keep quite happily for up to 2 weeks.

The syrups below will make 200ml. It is up to you how much to use on the cake base.

Rum Syrup

90g caster sugar
80ml water
30ml/2 tbsp dark rum
2 strips of unwaxed lemon zest

Espresso Syrup

60g/4 tbsp caster sugar
40ml/scant 3 tbsp water
100ml espresso
1 strip of orange zest

Autumn Spiced Syrup

100g demerara sugar
100ml water
1 star anise
2 cloves
2 cardamom pods
1 cinnamon stick

Lemon and Elderflower Syrup

100g caster sugar
100ml water
juice of 2 lemons
10g elderflower heads

Spreadables

I call these 'spreadables', but they can equally be fillings or inserts frozen inside a mousse.

All these recipes make 200g, or enough to spread on 1 sheet sponge (see page 144).

Caramelized White Chocolate Ganache

100g white chocolate
100ml double cream

Preheat the oven to 120°C fan/140°C/gas mark 1.

Chop the white chocolate into chunks and place on a baking tray.

Bake for 30 minutes until golden, smushing it around every 10 minutes with a rubber spatula. It may look like it is clumping up and hardening, but persist.

Decant into a heatproof container and allow to cool.

Warm the cream gently in a saucepan until steaming, then pour it over the caramelized white chocolate. Let it sit for 1 minute before stirring with a whisk from the centre to the outside (in order not to add air), until completely smooth.

Raspberry Caramel

100g caster sugar
30ml/2 tbsp water
60ml/4 tbsp raspberry purée
40g/scant 3 tbsp double cream

Put the caster sugar and measured water in a saucepan and place over a medium heat. Swirl the pan occasionally so each area receives the same amount of heat, but don't stir it.

When you have a light golden caramel, add the raspberry purée and cream, standing well back as it will splutter.

Let it bubble and then stir it together. When the purée and cream have dissolved, turn the heat off and allow to cool before using.

Red Berry Compote

160g fresh berries

40g/2½ tbsp caster sugar, or to taste

finely grated zest and juice of ½ unwaxed lemon

For the optional additions: use your palate and imagination to judge this!

cinnamon stick

vanilla pod

cardamom pods

Because we don't have the joy of berries all year round, here is a compote for you to utilize what you have around. Please taste the fruit before you cook it and add more sugar – or less – accordingly, as fresh fruit can really vary.

Place the berries and sugar in a saucepan and stir. Let this sit to macerate for 1 hour.

Warm gently over a low heat until the fruit breaks down and the compote bubbles gently.

Add the lemon zest and juice, and any optional additions, and stir over a low heat for a few minutes.

Remove from the heat. Carefully taste (it will be hot!) and adjust the sugar level if needed. Allow to cool before using.

Lime Curd

50g unsalted butter

50g caster sugar

50ml lime juice

1 egg

For the lime curd, heat together the butter and caster sugar in a saucepan. When the butter has melted, add the lime juice and stir well.

In a separate heatproof bowl, whisk the egg, then add the warmed butter mixture and whisk well.

Return to the heat and stir continuously with a spatula until thickened. Pour into a heatproof container and allow to cool before chilling in the fridge.

Hazelnut Praline Paste

120g caster sugar
100g blanched hazelnuts, roasted

Line a baking tray with baking paper.

In a saucepan over a medium heat, sprinkle in the sugar and let it melt until it turns into a golden caramel, without adding any water. Keep an eye on this, as it can turn dark and bitter in moments. Immediately pour it out onto the prepared tray when golden.

When it has cooled down, break it up into pieces and place into a blender with the roasted hazelnuts. Blitz for *ages* until it turns from a powder to a paste; do not be tempted to add oil! This should take around 20 minutes.

Salted Dark Chocolate Ganache

80g dark chocolate, chopped
100g double cream
20ml/1½ tbsp maple syrup
pinch of sea salt flakes

Place the dark chocolate in a large, heatproof bowl.

Warm the cream gently in a saucepan with the maple syrup until steaming, then pour it over the chopped chocolate. Let it sit for a minute, before stirring with a whisk from the centre to the outside (in order not to add air), until it is smooth and glossy. Finally, stir in the salt.

Keep aside ready to spread on the cake layers.

Mousses or fillers

These bits will be more substantial than the spreadables and make up a bigger part of your entremet. Here, I've suggested mousse, set creams and a buttercream. The buttercream would work better for something that is layered up, such as a gateau opera (see page 164), and the mousse for an entremet set into a silicone mould or glass.
 Each of these recipes makes 400–500g.

Crème Brûlée Custard

1 'platinum-grade' gelatine leaf
  (I use Dr. Oetker)
85g caster sugar
200ml double cream
150ml whole milk
1 vanilla pod, split lengthways,
  seeds scraped out
60g egg yolks

Soak the gelatine in ice-cold water in a small bowl.

Make a direct caramel by heating the sugar in a medium saucepan until it turns into a dark caramel. Turn the heat to low and pour in the cream and milk with the vanilla seeds. Bring to a gentle simmer.

Meanwhile, whisk the yolks together in a separate bowl.

When the cream mixture is starting to gently simmer, pour it over the yolks while whisking. Return to the heat and, using a spatula, cook until it is thick enough to coat the back of a wooden spoon.

When the gelatine is soft, squeeze out the excess water and stir into the caramel crème anglaise to dissolve.

Pour into a jug and allow to cool for 10 minutes at room temperature. The crème brûlée custard is now ready to be poured into a glass and set (it will need a minimum of 4 hours in the fridge), or poured into a silicone mould and frozen overnight for an entremet insert.

For the tart of dreams (see page 171), use a mini half-sphere silicon mould and pour the custard into 16 of the holes (to make 8 full spheres) before freezing them. You will have more custard than you need for this so, as I've suggested above, set the leftover custard in a glass and eat it as it is, or keep it frozen for another day.

Coffee Buttercream

60ml water

140g caster sugar

2 eggs (ideally 150g)

1 tbsp instant coffee

200g unsalted butter, softened, cubed

pinch of salt

For the coffee buttercream, place the measured water and sugar into a saucepan over a medium heat. We are taking the sugar to 121°C, so keep a thermometer in it.

Start gently whipping the eggs in a stand mixer until pale and frothy.

When the sugar reaches 119°C, remove it from the heat (the residual heat from the pan will help it climb to 121°C by the time it gets to the mixer).

Gently pour this sugar syrup in a stream down the side of the bowl with the mixer on medium speed, being careful not to let the stream touch the whisk. Whisk on medium speed and add the instant coffee. Whip until cool; the bowl should not feel hot to touch.

Start adding the butter in chunks while the machine is still going. Once all the butter has been added, whisk until combined then add a pinch of salt.

Switch the whisk attachment for the paddle attachment and mix for a further few minutes. Keep in a bowl on the side, do not refrigerate before spreading onto the cake.

Coconut and Bay Whipped Panna Cotta

150ml double cream

300ml coconut milk

3 bay leaves

4 'platinum-grade' gelatine leaves (I use Dr. Oetker)

75g caster sugar

Warm the milk and cream in a saucepan with the bay leaves until just warmed, then take off the heat, cover and allow to infuse for 2 hours.

Strain this and re-weigh the liquid, topping it up to 450ml with extra cream if needed.

Soak the gelatine leaves in ice-cold water in a bowl.

Warm the infused cream and milk together with the caster sugar until steaming, then remove from the heat.

Squeeze out the excess water from the gelatine leaves and stir into the warmed cream mixture until dissolved. Pour into a heatproof container and allow to cool before placing in the fridge for a minimum of 4 hours, ideally overnight.

When the mixture has softly set, you can whip it. This changes the texture from soft and jelly-like to aerated, light and smooth. Gently whip on a medium speed until thickened, like softly whipped cream. The gelatine acts to stabilize it.

When it has thickened use it to spread over the sponge.

Caramelized Chocolate Mousse

3 'platinum-grade' gelatine leaves
(I use Dr. Oetker)
10ml/2 tsp water
45g caster sugar
60g double cream, plus 200g
40ml whole milk
40g egg yolks
180g milk chocolate, chopped
1g/large pinch of sea salt flakes

Soak the gelatine in ice-cold water in a bowl.

Make a caramel by heating the measured water and sugar together in a saucepan, shaking the pan gently if needed so it colours evenly, until the sugar turns to a dark caramel.

Stand back and pour in the 60g cream and the milk gently, it will bubble. Stir gently until it's all as one. Pour the caramel over the egg yolks in a large heatproof bowl and whisk quickly. Return this to the saucepan and cook over a low heat, stirring with a silicone spatula, until it is thick enough to coat the back of the spatula.

Remove from the heat. Squeeze out the excess water from the gelatine and stir into the caramel crème anglaise.

Place the chopped milk chocolate in a large heatproof bowl. Pour the warm crème anglaise mixture over the chopped milk chocolate and stir with a whisk to melt. Allow to cool until no longer warm to the touch.

Whip the 200g of cream to soft peaks. Fold the cream into the chocolate mixture, using a whisk to make sure there are no lumps, adding the salt at the same time.

The mousse is now ready to be set. We will be pouring this into half-sphere moulds and inserting the crème brûlée custard.

Passion Fruit and Greek Yogurt Mousse

3 'platinum grade' gelatine leaves
(I use Dr. Oetker)
200g double cream
130ml passion fruit purée
60g caster sugar
110g Greek yogurt

Soak the gelatine in ice-cold water in a small bowl.

Heat the cream and passion fruit purée together with the sugar in a saucepan. When it's steaming, take it off the heat.

Squeeze out the excess water from the gelatine and stir it into the warm purée until dissolved.

Pour over the yogurt in a heatproof bowl and stir with a whisk.

Allow to cool briefly before pouring into moulds and chilling in the fridge, or freezing overnight in silicone moulds.

Glazes or Garnishes

It is up to you whether you want to use a glaze or not. Typically, if you had set entremets in layers into glasses, you wouldn't need a glaze. A glaze is more to pour over something frozen to give it a shine. If you have been cleverly putting together an entremet in a silicone mould with lots of fun layers, unmould it and place it on a wire rack with a tray underneath. Make sure the tray has a lip, to catch the glaze that will inevitably run off. Working quickly, pour the warmed glaze over the entremet in one go before transferring it to a plate and popping it in the fridge. As it defrosts, the glaze will keep the whole thing intact and looking *flawless*.

As an alternative, you can also top your entremets with Italian meringue (as we did for the tropical roulade, page 168) and then torch it. That's the type of thing you do for friends who like drama.

The glazes here make 200–300g, enough for 1 large entremet.

Torched Meringue

120g caster sugar
40ml water
60g egg whites

Place the sugar and measured water in a saucepan and swirl gently so the water covers the sugar. Place over a gentle heat until the sugar dissolves, then add a sugar thermometer. When the sugar reaches 110°C, start whisking the egg whites in a stand mixer on a medium speed.

When the whites are frothy and thick, the sugar should be at 118°C. Remove from the heat and let the syrup settle for a few seconds before pouring it down the side of the egg white bowl, still beating, making sure the stream of syrup doesn't touch the whisk. Whisk on a medium speed until the bowl has cooled and the meringue is thick.

Spoon it on top of your finished cake and **TORCH** it, honey.

Fruit Jelly

2½ 'platinum-grade' gelatine
    leaves (I use Dr. Oetker)
200ml fruit purée of your choice
25g caster sugar
juice of 1 lemon

Soak the gelatine in ice-cold water in a bowl.

Heat the fruit purée with the sugar and lemon juice until dissolved.
Squeeze out the excess water from the gelatine before whisking it into
the purée mixture off the heat.

Allow to cool before re-warming to use at pouring consistency.

Yogurt Glaze

1 'platinum-grade' gelatine leaf
    (I use Dr. Oetker)
100g double cream
50g glucose syrup
70g white chocolate, chopped
100g Greek yogurt

Soak the gelatine in ice-cold water in a bowl.

Heat the cream and glucose together until the glucose has fully melted.
Squeeze out the water from the gelatine, add it to the cream mix and
stir to dissolve.

Put the white chocolate in a heatproof bowl, pour over the cream
mixture and stir to melt. When this is around 30°C, add the yogurt and
stir to combine, then refrigerate overnight (or for up to
5 days). It is now ready to use.

Chocolate Magic Shell

Makes about 370g

225g good-quality dark
    chocolate
150ml flavourless oil
½ tsp sea salt

Melt the chocolate in a bain-marie, take it off the heat and then slowly
pour in the oil while stirring to combine. If you need to, you can use a
hand blender to emulsify.

Stir in the salt and use the mixture when it's at body temperature – too
hot and it will melt your creations. Leave at room temperature. You can
keep a container of this out at room temperature during service and it
will last really nicely. The mixture will keep in the fridge in an airtight
container for 1 week. Just warm and then cool it slightly to use again.

Crunchy Bits

All crunchy and crispy baked things – of whatever nature – should be stored in an airtight container to retain their texture. These crispy things are great for sprinkling between layers of cake, or crushing and folding through mousse or freshly churned ice cream. Take them and run wild!

All these recipes make 200g.

Sweet and Salty Peanuts

130g salted peanuts
80g caster sugar
30ml/2 tbsp water

Preheat the oven to 150°C fan/170°C/gas mark 3½.

Roast the peanuts on a baking tray for 10–12 minutes. Line another baking tray with baking paper.

When the nuts are nearly ready, place the sugar and measured water in a saucepan and bring to a rolling boil. Before it caramelizes, add the hot nuts and stir, stir, stir. They will turn from sandy to caramelized with a bit of persistence, but reduce the heat if it gets a bit much.

Pour onto the prepared tray and allow to cool, before smashing up and using.

Spiced Crumble

90g plain flour
¼ tsp ground ginger
¼ tsp ground cinnamon
⅛ tsp bicarbonate of soda
pinch of fine salt
35g demerara sugar
75g unsalted butter, cold and
    cubed

Preheat the oven to 170°C fan/190°C/gas mark 5.

In a large bowl, stir together all the dry ingredients.

Add the cubed butter and, using your fingertips or a stand mixer fitted with the paddle attachment, mix to the texture of crumbs.

Tip onto a baking tray and bake for 25 minutes, stirring once or twice during baking to move the browner edges into the centre.

Remove from the oven and, while still warm, crush with a fork, then allow to cool.

Coconut Meringue Strips

70g egg whites
130g caster sugar
20–30g desiccated coconut

Preheat the oven – with no fan – to 100°C/gas mark ½. In a large bowl, whisk the egg white until frothy, then gradually add the sugar, whisking continually, until stiff peaks form.

Spoon into a piping bag fitted with a round 1cm (½in) nozzle and pipe lines onto a baking tray lined with baking paper.

Sprinkle liberally with the desiccated coconut.

Bake for 1–1½ hours, or until the dried-out strips will lift off the paper cleanly.

Popcorn and Rosemary Caramel

90g caster sugar
7g rosemary leaves
10g/¾ tbsp unsalted butter
120g popcorn
1g/large pinch of sea salt flakes

Line a baking tray with baking paper, or find a silicone mat.

Heat the sugar gently in a saucepan, lightly shaking the pan if needed so it heats evenly, until a golden caramel forms. Add the rosemary and stir. Whisk in the butter, then stir in the popcorn and salt.

Tip onto the prepared tray or silicone mat and leave to cool.

Cacao Nib Tuiles

85g unsalted butter
70g caster sugar
30ml water
40g plain flour
20g cacao nibs

Preheat the oven to 160°C fan/180°C/gas mark 4 and line a baking tray with baking paper.

Place the butter, sugar and measured water in a saucepan and bring to the boil. Simmer gently until it turns into a golden caramel. Remove from the heat and stir in the flour and cacao nibs.

Spread onto the prepared tray as thinly as possible.

Bake for 7–12 minutes, until golden and bubbly. Take out of the oven and allow to cool before snapping into shards.

Sourdough Crumbs

150g mix of white and brown
sourdough bread
75g dark brown sugar
20ml water

Preheat the oven to 140°C fan/160°C/gas mark 3.

Cut the crusts off the bread. Take the crumb of the bread and rip it apart into a food processor bowl. Blitz into pieces that are a bit bigger than breadcrumbs.

Place them into a large baking tray and mix through the sugar, splash the measured water over and mix it up. The breadcrumbs should be lying in a single layer.

Bake for 30–40 minutes, stirring every 10 minutes. The aim is to dry them out, they will crisp up more once cool. These can always be revived in the oven again if needed.

'Granola'

60g unsalted butter
50g golden syrup or honey
80g jumbo oats
50g bran flakes cereal
60g skin-on almonds
15g/1 tbsp pumpkin seeds
15g/1 tbsp sesame seeds
pinch of sea salt flakes

Use this as your base, but feel free to change the nuts to suit you, or add a citrus zest, or change the cereal.

Preheat the oven to 165°C fan/180°C/gas mark 4.

Melt the butter and golden syrup together in a saucepan over a gentle heat until completely liquid.

In a large bowl, mix all the dry ingredients together. Stir in the warmed butter mixture evenly.

Tip onto a large baking tray, big enough that the mixture can lie in a single layer – this will help it to bake evenly. Bake for 10 minutes, then remove from the oven and stir. Return to the oven for a further 5–7 minutes until golden, then stir and leave to cool completely before breaking up and using.

Fruit Crisps

50g caster sugar

50ml water

juice of 1 lemon

200g pear, pineapple, apple or other fruit of your choice

I've used a sugar syrup here, but you can also leave it out and simply brush the fruit slices with lemon juice instead.

Place the sugar and water in a saucepan and heat until the sugar has dissolved completely, then squeeze in the lemon juice and allow to cool.

Preheat the oven to 100°C fan/120°C/gas mark ½.

Finely slice the fruit of your choice on a mandoline to almost paper-thin.

Brush the sugar syrup solution over both sides of each fruit slice and lay it flat on a baking tray lined with baking paper.

Place the tray in the oven for the fruit to completely dry out. After 1 hour, turn the tray around and bake for a further 30–60 minutes, checking the fruit slices frequently. As soon as they are completely dried out, remove them from the oven.

Crystallized White Chocolate

120g caster sugar

30ml/2 tbsp water

70g white chocolate, chopped

Line a baking tray with baking paper, or find a silicone mat.

Put the sugar and measured water in a saucepan over a medium heat and stir, then bring to a simmer. Add a sugar thermometer. Take the sugar to 130°C, then remove from the heat. Immediately tip in the chopped chocolate and stir with a whisk until crumbs form.

Tip onto the prepared tray or silicone mat and allow to cool before using.

Something to Get You Started

Over the next few pages you will find three of my suggestions for stunning, complete entremets. Give them a go; they are really great examples of how to build a entremet using all of the elements listed, pairing together flavours and textures to create a show-stopping dessert. You'll find an over-the-top opera cake that will feed 16! A tropical roulade that will tick every citrus lover's box and a very fancy tart of dreams.

OTT Opera Cake

Here I'm showing you how to layer up a cake with different elements by upping the components of a traditional gateau opera, a classic coffee and chocolate cake originating in France. It just so happens to be one of my all-time favourites.

Notice that here you will need more quantities of some of the recipes to cover the large sheets of sponge (it makes a large cake, enough for 16). To make this, you will need the following:

1 X ALMOND JACONDE SPONGE
1 X LIGHT FLOURLESS CHOCOLATE CAKE
1 X ROASTED PEANUT AND MALT SPONGE
2 X COFFEE BUTTERCREAM
2 X SALTED DARK CHOCOLATE GANACHE
3 X ESPRESSO SYRUP
1 X CHOCOLATE MAGIC SHELL

To assemble:

Have all of your elements ready.

Place the chocolate sponge on a large tray lined with baking paper – this will help you to transfer the cake once assembled. Brush one-third of the syrup over the chocolate sponge. Spread half of the ganache over the sponge and put in the fridge for 5 minutes to set.

Remove from the fridge and spread over half of the coffee buttercream.

Place the peanut sponge on top and brush with another third of the syrup.

Spread over the second half of the coffee buttercream, then return to the fridge for 5 minutes to set.

Top with the almond sponge, using the last third of the syrup to soak the cake.

Spread over the second half of the ganache and place the whole cake in the fridge for 1 hour to set completely.

Put a wire rack over a baking tray with a lip and transfer the cold cake onto the wire rack, removing the baking paper.

Bring the chocolate magic shell back to a gentle heat so it's only very slightly warm, but pourable.

Pour all over the cake and leave to drip for 5 minutes before using a large palette knife to transfer the cake to a clean large chopping board.

Place in the fridge for another 10 minutes before using a sharp knife to slice; then trim off the edges to expose that gorgeous layering!

Tropical Roulade

This is a great way of turning one of those sheet sponges into a fancy roulade – we are going tropical/refreshing here. Once the roulade has been assembled and tightly wrapped, it can also be frozen for 30 days: simply defrost fully before topping with meringue and torching.

1 X MANGO AND LIME SPONGE
2 X LIME CURD
1 X COCONUT WHIPPED PANNA COTTA
1 X TORCHED MERINGUE
+ FRESHLY SLICED MANGO

To assemble

Place the mango and lime sponge on a baking tray with baking paper underneath, this will help you to roll the sponge.

Spread three-quarters of the lime curd all over the sponge evenly.

Spread over the whipped panna cotta.

Evenly place sliced mango pieces on the sponge.

Dot the remaining curd over the mango pieces (optional).

Place this tray in the fridge for 10 minutes.

Using the paper to assist you, roll the sponge up widthways until it is a roulade shape.

Take this roulade and place it onto a large sheet of clingfilm, use the clingfilm to wrap the roulade tightly to form a sausage shape.

Place in the fridge for 1 hour.

Remove the roulade from the fridge, remove the clingfilm and baking paper and place onto a tray, dollop the meringue over the top and blowtorch before serving.

Chocolate, Caramel Tart of Dreams

All the flavours and textures in this creation make it the tart of my dreams, and I hope it becomes yours too. It makes eight 8cm (3¼in) tartlets.

1 X SHORT CHOCOLATE AND PEANUT PASTRY
1 X FLOURLESS CHOCOLATE CAKE
1 X RUM SYRUP
1 X HAZELNUT PRALINE (WE USED HALF A BATCH BUT IT'S BEST
    TO MAKE A FULL ONE)
1 X CRÈME BRÛLÉE CUSTARD
1 X CARAMELIZED CHOCOLATE MOUSSE
1 X MAGIC SHELL
+ CRÈME FRAÎCHE

To assemble

Remove the frozen crème brûlée custard from the mini half sphere moulds and stick the 16 halves together, to make 8 full spheres. If you just push them together they will stick on their own.

Pour the caramelized chocolate mousse into a larger half sphere mould, then insert a crème brûlée custard sphere into the middle. Level the top off with a palette knife and freeze overnight.

The next day, brush the short chocolate and peanut pastry tart cases with some melted cocoa butter or white chocolate to keep them snappy, this is optional. Allow to set before using.

Put 1 teaspoon of hazelnut praline paste in the bottom of each tart shell.

Cut eight 5cm (2in) circles out of the flourless chocolate cake, brush with rum syrup, place this sponge on top of the praline in the pastry.

Pipe crème fraîche around the edges of the sponge and on top, level with a small palette knife.

Demould the large spheres of mousse onto a wire rack with a tray underneath, then pour over the magic shell – it will set in seconds. Using a small palette knife, transfer this to sit on top of the tart. Place the tarts in the fridge for 4 hours, which gives them time to defrost. If needed lightly blowtorch the tops before serving with shavings of dark chocolate.

Ice C
Ice C
Ice C
Ice C

ream

ream

ream

ream

Ice cream has the ability to incite a lot of joy.

You lot really love the stuff! As do I. This chapter is dedicated to ice cream that comes out best when churned in a machine. Sorry to say it, but if you want parfait or sorbet, go back to my first book mate! This is pure ice cream.

Do you remember the first time you ate ice cream? No? Neither do I. What I do know is that I'm an ice cream gal, I want **ALL** of the frozen, dense-yet-light fatty air. Ice lollies, yeah they're cool but I will almost always choose the decadent option over the lighter one.

As a child I thought the pinnacle of wealth was getting an ice cream cake on your birthday. I have yet to be given one; in fact, I often get asked by my mum to make my own birthday cake. I think you're either one of those people that **REALLY** loves ice cream and thinks about opening your own ice cream shop on the reg, or you're just a bit unfazed by it. I'm obviously in the first camp, meaning I've spent quite a lot of money on various ice cream machines and will happily spend hours testing and eating the stuff in my kitchen.

Ice cream has the ability to incite a lot of joy; does anyone else remember eating a Viennetta with your KFC? Or when McDonald's would serve you an apple pie and ice cream

TOGETHER? Joy! Every Tuesday for over 10 years straight my mum would have to take me to ballet class after school in her little battered Micra and, as a bribe, we would get ice cream in the summer from the off license, or a McDonald's in winter in the hour between. That logic still continues with the way I view fitness: fitness – sure, I love being active, but I also have no qualms with eating an ice cream, a pizza or some fried chicken straight after.

I remember my mum having a battle with our local ice cream van man for parking outside our house after school had finished – we'd soon get a rush of kids on our drive with ice cream wrappers everywhere. I remember feeling so mortified at the thought of upsetting the most important man in the area, jeopardizing my chance of eating a 99p flake. Thankfully, I am now old enough to argue with the ice cream man and then use my own money to buy a box of flakes from the shop to dip into my own homemade ice cream. How I have grown.

A NOTE: All the recipes in this chapter make between 900ml and 1.1 litres (1½ and 1¾ pints), depending on how well you scrape out the ice-cream machine.

Miso Caramel

This ice cream sits on the edge of salty and sweet in a mouth-tingling way. The miso caramel adds a real depth of flavour and gives the ice cream a very smooth texture. If you don't have time to churn this, I also recommend either serving it warm as a custard with a dessert, or, if you're like Sam Tucker, my ice cream recipe tester, drink it straight-up!

For the ice cream
260ml whole milk
400g double cream
80g caster sugar
6 egg yolks
a pinch of sea salt flakes

For the miso caramel
70g caster sugar
15g/1 tbsp unsalted butter
130g double cream
50g white miso

To make the caramel, place a saucepan over a medium heat, sprinkle in the sugar and let it make a dark caramel, swirling the pan occasionally to distribute the heat evenly, but not stirring.

Add the butter and whisk well. Stand back, pour in the cream and let it bubble for a minute, then remove from the heat and whisk in the miso. Set aside. When it has cooled slightly, pour it into a heatproof dish and allow to cool. We want it to be at pouring consistency but not *hot*.

For the ice cream, heat the milk, cream and half the sugar in a medium saucepan until steaming.

Meanwhile, whisk the egg yolks with the second half of the sugar.

Pour the steaming milk mixture over the yolk mixture and whisk well, then return the custard to the pan and, using a spatula, stir constantly over a medium heat until it coats the back of a spoon.

Remove from the heat and add all but 2 tbsp of the miso caramel, whisking well, or blending with a stick blender. Pass through a sieve, transfer to a clean container and allow to cool before chilling in the fridge overnight.

Whisk in the salt, then churn in an ice-cream machine according to the manufacturer's instructions. At the last minute, swirl through the remaining miso caramel.

Bran Flake and Milk Chocolate

Every night, without fail, Biji soaks her bran flakes in milk ready to drench again with freshly made chai in the morning for breakfast. We don't know why she does this or where she got the idea from, but she's fixed on it. The chai must be served at the right temperature in the same metal mug, with the cereal in the same deep bowl, along with the same metal spoon. Every day is groundhog day via soaked bran flakes.

Initially, I wanted to make a toasted spelt and milk chocolate ice cream. But during testing late at night I watched Biji soak her bran flakes and, at the same time, decided to do the same – but with milk chocolate – for ice cream. The spelt version was very good, but the bran flake recipe was the clear winner.

500ml whole milk, plus extra
  if needed
120g bran flakes cereal
330g double cream
145g caster sugar
5 egg yolks
80g milk chocolate, chopped

Warm the milk until it's warm to the touch, then add the bran flakes and set aside for 30 minutes. Strain – you should be left with roughly 300ml; if not, top it up with a bit of extra milk.

Heat the infused milk, cream and half the sugar in a medium saucepan until steaming.

Meanwhile, whisk the egg yolks with the second half of the sugar.

Pour the steaming milk mixture over the yolk mixture and whisk well, then return it to the pan and, using a spatula, stir constantly over a medium heat until the custard coats the back of a spoon.

Remove from the heat and add the milk chocolate, whisking well or blending in with a stick blender until the chocolate melts, then pass through a sieve. Transfer to a clean container and allow to cool before chilling in the fridge overnight.

Churn in an ice-cream machine according to the manufacturer's instructions.

Peanut Butter and Raspberry with Chocolate

Most people like peanut butter and raspberry, don't they? The peanut butter base here is really addictive. Use deep, dark, good-quality peanut butter for the best results and offset it with a sharp raspberry jam – seeds or not, you decide!

The chocolate magic shell is optional, but it's a lot of fun, simply pour it over scooped ice cream and watch it set in seconds to form a set layer that contrasts texturally with the soft, smooth ice cream.

260ml whole milk

480g double cream

100g caster sugar

6 egg yolks

60g honey

160g dark roast peanut butter

sea salt flakes

100g raspberry jam

Chocolate Magic Shell (see page 155), optional

Heat the milk, cream and half the sugar in a medium saucepan until steaming.

Meanwhile, whisk the egg yolks with the second half of the sugar and the honey.

Pour the steaming milk mixture over the yolk mixture and whisk well, then return the mixture to the pan and, using a spatula, stir constantly over a medium heat until the custard coats the back of a spoon.

Remove from the heat and add the peanut butter, whisking well or blending in with a stick blender, then pass through a sieve and add the salt.

Transfer to a clean container and allow to cool before chilling in the fridge overnight.

Churn in an ice-cream machine according to the manufacturer's instructions. Swirl in the raspberry jam once churned. Chill in the freezer before topping with magic shell, if using.

Coconut and Lime

This is a really refreshing one. Any leftover lime curd can be kept in the fridge for up to three days and used elsewhere (I've used it in the Tropical Roulade entremet, see page 168). It's punchy and beautiful next to the silky coconut ice cream.

200g double cream
25g liquid glucose
100g caster sugar
30g cornflour
400ml coconut milk
160g coconut cream
2g/½ tsp fine salt
1 quantity Lime Curd (see page 149)

Heat the cream and the liquid glucose in a saucepan.

Stir together the sugar and cornflour in a bowl. Whisk this into the warmed cream mixture and continue to whisk over a medium heat until bubbling and slightly thickened. Pour into a blender with the coconut milk, coconut cream and salt. Blitz well.

Pour into a container and chill in the fridge overnight.

Churn in an ice-cream machine according to the manufacturer's instructions. Swirl in the lime curd once churned.

Mango

While writing this book, I spent a lot of time around my mum, who would throw out suggestions whenever she could (most of the time very unhelpful). Whenever I asked her what her favourite flavour – of anything – was, her response was always the same: 'mango'. She doesn't tire of them, and it should come as no surprise that she chose mango as her favourite ice cream flavour... not sorbet, mind you, ice cream. If my mum were to write a cookbook, I think it would be called *100 Ways With Mango*.

375g Kesar mango purée
375ml double cream
6 egg yolks (about 20g each)
45g caster sugar
juice of 2 limes
pinch of salt

Heat the mango purée and cream in a medium saucepan until steaming.

Meanwhile, whisk the egg yolks with the sugar.

Pour the steaming cream mixture over the yolk mixture and whisk well, then return the mixture to the pan and, using a spatula, stir constantly over a medium heat until the custard coats the back of a spoon.

Remove from the heat and add the lime juice and salt, whisking well or blending in with a stick blender, then pass through a sieve.

Transfer to a clean container and allow to cool before chilling in the fridge overnight.

Churn in an ice-cream machine according to the manufacturer's instructions.

lated

serts

ated

serts

We make desserts for people we love.

Professional kitchens can be tense places: there are often a lot of egos involved, as well as pent-up emotion and energy that can spill out in ways that most people would deem unacceptable in the workplace. There's a multitude of factors that could explain why this is, but the reason why it often *continues* is because of a lack of awareness of how important a strong leader is. So there begins a vicious circle of poor leaders breeding poor leaders. The so-called 'soft skills' aren't always taught or given enough credit, but they can really make or break a kitchen. I think of teams and the culture of any working environment as a bit of a chain. You simply cannot want to open a food business – or any business that involves people – without considering… the people part.

The restaurant world can be fickle. We see restaurants open their shiny new doors and disappear within a few years, only to be replaced by the next equally shiny, hopeful venture. One of the biggest keys to opening a sustainable restaurant with longevity is the staff. Happy staff provide loyalty, and loyalty ensures consistency; in turn, consistency is key to maintaining a returning customer base. A fruitful, returning customer base keeps the doors open.

Working to listen to the needs of employees and striving to cultivate a healthy work environment can make or break a business, and I believe it's one of the most essential parts of running a restaurant and why I started Countertalk. Equally, as an employee, it's really important to respect and understand the owner's perspective: it takes a lot to open a place and stand in the thick of it.

I've got a real love for restaurants. It was through working in restaurants that I learned so much, not only about food and flavour, but about people. Working in service and making desserts to order is a big part of the fun and thrill of life in a professional kitchen. It involves striving hard to make sure each element is ready and that the whole is as efficiently organized as possible. Making a dessert to order, or plating a dessert with a few different elements, allows you to experiment and requires an audience. A soufflé is the perfect example of this: imagine whipping up a few chocolate soufflés at a dinner party with an accompanying batch of home-made ice cream!

We make desserts for **PEOPLE**, whether that's for eager customers or for those we love, as well as to mark significant milestones in life. Eating something sweet isn't about survival as such, but it does make life a whole lot better. In this last chapter we are going to explore a few options for plated desserts, a part of the pastry world that I love so much.

Soufflé

I think it's important that we directly address the concept of a soufflé here in three separate ways. One that can be made dairy-free with a thickened cornflour base (the raspberry); a more traditional version with a crème pât base (the chocolate); and soufflé pancakes for fun. I want **YOU** to have a go at making at least one of these, to really prove to yourself that you **CAN** make a soufflé.

Raspberry Soufflé

Makes 2–3 medium ramekins

For the soufflés

200g raspberries

40g caster sugar, plus 20g, plus extra for the ramekins

5g/1 tsp cornflour

2 egg whites (60g in total)

softened unsalted butter, for the ramekins

icing sugar, for dusting

For the pistachio custard

250g double cream

250ml whole milk

60g caster sugar

3 egg yolks

20g pistachio praline paste

Start by making the fruit base for the soufflés, which can be made in advance and chilled in the fridge. Blitz the raspberries in a food processor and pass them through a sieve to achieve a purée.

In a bowl, mix together the 40g caster sugar and the cornflour.

Pour the purée into a saucepan and warm gently. When it's steaming, add the cornflour mixture and whisk well. Cook for 3–4 minutes over a medium-low heat. It will bubble, so keep whisking.

Take off the heat and pour into a heatproof container, then chill in the fridge until cool.

For the pistachio custard, heat the cream and milk together in a saucepan with half the sugar.

In a bowl, whisk the second half of the sugar with the egg yolks.

Pour the steaming milk over the yolk mixture and whisk well, then return to a low heat and cook gently, stirring continuously with a spatula, until the custard coats the back of a spoon.

Raspberry Soufflé

Remove from the heat, add the pistachio praline paste, whisking well or blending in with a stick blender, then pass through a sieve. Allow to cool before chilling in the fridge.

To make the soufflés, liberally butter 2 large or 3 small ramekins with softened butter, brushing in upward motions. Add a spoon of caster sugar and swirl the ramekins to coat, tapping out the excess. Place in the fridge.

Preheat the oven to 170°C fan/190°C/gas mark 5.

Whisk the egg whites in a clean bowl until soft peaks form, then add the 20g sugar, a little at a time, whisking constantly, until the mixture is stiff and glossy meringue.

Put the raspberry mixture in a large bowl and beat it down. Fold in the meringue in three batches; take care to do this gently, as the mixture should remain voluminous and delicate.

Fill the ramekins with the soufflé mixture. Tap them gently on the work surface, then smooth over the tops with a palette knife and run your thumb around the inside edges to create a rim.

Place the ramekins on a baking tray and bake for 12–14 minutes until well risen.

Dust the tops with icing sugar and serve immediately with the cold pistachio custard.

Roasted Hazelnut Soufflé with Chocolate Sauce

I want to reassure you that a soufflé is not scary. Think of it simply as a thickened base, here a crème pâtissière, with a simple French meringue folded through it. Not that difficult, see? The rise on this is a thing of beauty and it is like eating a fluffy Ferrero Rocher, a true crowd-pleaser. Serve at a dinner party to impress, if the dining table isn't too far a walk from the kitchen... You can make the hazelnut base in advance and keep it in the fridge for up to 3 days. Just make sure you loosen it properly before folding the meringue through it.

Makes 4 medium ramekins

For the hazelnut crème pâtissière
40g blanched hazelnuts
180ml whole milk
40g caster sugar
10g/2 tsp cornflour
pinch of fine salt
15g/1 tbsp plain flour
40g egg yolks (2 large egg yolks)

For the soufflé mixture
50g softened unsalted butter, plus extra for the ramekins
20g cocoa powder or grated chocolate
180g egg whites
60g caster sugar

For the chocolate sauce
90g dark chocolate, chopped
40g water, plus extra if needed
1 tbsp demerara sugar
pinch of sea salt flakes

Preheat the oven to 150°C fan/170°C/gas mark 3½.

Start by preparing a hazelnut butter. Roast the hazelnuts on a baking tray for 10–15 minutes until golden. Allow to cool. Blitz the roasted hazelnuts in a powerful blender to form a smooth butter.

Heat the milk with the sugar and the hazelnut butter in a saucepan over a gentle heat and mix well.

Whisk the cornflour, salt and plain flour together separately.

Place the yolks in another large bowl and whisk to break them up. Slowly add the cornflour mixture and whisk really well; it will feel quite dry so, if needed, add a splash of the warmed milk. We want to avoid lumps here.

Once all of the cornflour mixture is combined with the yolks, gently pour the warm milk over the yolks, whisking until smooth.

Return to the saucepan and whisk over a medium heat until thickened and bubbling (a few minutes). Remove from the heat and carefully place in a blender. Blitz well. (A hand blender also works here.)

Pour the hazelnut crème pâtissière into a heatproof container and place a sheet of clingfilm or baking paper directly on top. Allow to cool, then refrigerate to chill thoroughly for an hour.

Roasted Hazelnut Soufflé with Chocolate Sauce

To serve
30g grated dark chocolate
20g roasted hazelnuts, crushed

Liberally butter 4 medium ramekins with softened butter, making sure you coat the whole thing well, brushing in upward motions. Chill in the fridge for 10 minutes. Remove from the fridge and butter again. Add the cocoa powder or grated chocolate and swirl the ramekin to coat, tap out the excess, then return to the fridge.

Preheat the oven to 170°C fan/190°C/gas mark 5.

Make a French meringue by whisking the egg whites with the caster sugar in a clean bowl to soft peaks.

Scoop the chilled hazelnut crème pâtissière into the bowl of a stand mixer fitted with the paddle attachment, then beat down gently to soften it. We do this so the meringue folds in easier with fewer lumps or pockets of meringue.

Fold in the meringue in three batches; take care to do this gently, as the mixture should remain voluminous and delicate.

Fill the ramekins with the soufflé mixture, tapping them down gently on a work surface. Smooth over the top with a palette knife and run your thumb around the inside edge. Place the ramekins on a baking tray and bake for 12 minutes.

Meanwhile, make the chocolate sauce by putting the chocolate, water and sugar in a saucepan and heating gently, stirring frequently. As soon as a smooth sauce forms, remove from the heat and stir in the salt. This sauce can be served cool or warm, if it needs loosening feel free to add another splash of water while reheating, as it's very forgiving.

Remove the soufflés from the oven and dust the tops with grated chocolate and a handful of crushed hazelnuts.

When serving, allow guests to make a hole in the middle of the soufflé to pour in the chocolate sauce.

Soufflé Pancakes with Berries

These feel quite special to me. They were one of the technical challenges on *Junior Bake Off*. Firstly, I can't believe I was asked to be a judge on **THAT** show. You know how I got approached? Through an Instagram DM!

The food producer, Jonathan Scrafton, who I had the pleasure of meeting on the show, toyed with this idea for soufflé pancakes with me and – after a bit of back and forth – we settled on a cat-shaped mould. It was such a fun challenge and really and truly the bakers did very well with it.

These are so delicious eaten for breakfast, if you're aiming to impress, or even after dinner as they are very light. You will need 5–6 metal rings, each 9cm (3½in) in diameter and 5cm (2in) deep.

Makes 5–6

2 large eggs
15ml/1 tbsp neutral oil, plus extra for greasing
¼ tsp vanilla extract
2 tbsp whole milk
50g plain flour
pinch of salt
1 tbsp cornflour
1 tsp baking powder
45g caster sugar
30ml warm water

To serve

icing sugar
seasonal fruit compote

Separate the eggs and place the egg yolks into one large bowl and the whites in another.

Whisk the oil with the yolks, vanilla extract and milk.

In a separate bowl, stir together the flour, salt, cornflour and baking powder.

Sift the dry ingredients over the yolk mixture and whisk in well.

Whisk the egg whites until soft peaks form, then whisk in the sugar, a little at a time, whisking constantly until the mixture is stiff and glossy. Fold this gently into the egg yolk mixture.

Grease 5–6 metal rings, each 9cm (3½in) in diameter and 5cm (2in) deep, with oil. Take a deep frying pan (with a lid) and set it over a medium heat. Lightly oil the pan and put the rings in. Fill each one with batter to just over halfway.

Cook over a medium heat until bubbles start to appear on the surface.

Pour the warm water down the edge of the pan, so it runs outside the rings, and place the lid on top. Reduce the heat to low and steam for 8 minutes.

Remove the lid; the water should have evaporated now. Flip the pancakes over to brown the other sides briefly.

Remove the pancakes from the rings, sift over icing sugar and serve with seasonal fruit compote (see page 149).

Rhubarb Moonshine with White Chocolate and Lychees

This is not for everyone and I would say it is perfect for someone who doesn't quite want a dessert, but may want to dip their toe in. This person might like spirits, wine and sharp fruits but not chocolate, custard or cream. Maybe you make this for someone who loves fruit and not dessert... to make them feel included at a dinner party. Maybe it's for that fussy customer who books a table every Monday evening at 8.15pm sharp, who is on a dairy-free diet (minus the chocolate sauce, obvs).

A moonshine, as I'm going to call it, is essentially a whipped jelly, made by making a jelly base and whipping it as it cools. Texturally it tastes fizzy and cloud-like, carrying the flavour in one of its purest forms. I first watched Rosy Rong, a chef at St. JOHN, make this *by hand* one afternoon. It took forever. You can use an electric whisk or a stand mixer.

This is a lot of fun. I think you should make it, because you've already come this far.

Rhubarb Moonshine with White Chocolate and Lychees

Makes 6

For the rhubarb moonshine
400g forced rhubarb
100g caster sugar, plus extra if needed
400ml water
juice of ½ lime, plus extra if needed
2½ 'platinum grade' gelatine leaves (I use Dr. Oetker)

For the white chocolate sauce (optional)
200g white chocolate
200ml double cream
½ vanilla pod, split lengthways, seeds scraped out

To garnish
fresh lychees
poached rhubarb

Preheat the oven to 160°C fan/180°C/gas mark 4.

Cut the rhubarb into 5cm (2in) pieces, removing the stems and the stalks. Wash and place into a large deep roasting tin. Sprinkle over the sugar and pour in the water. Stir, before placing into an oven for 12 minutes, or until the rhubarb is slightly softened but still a touch firm in the middle.

Remove from the oven and allow to cool before placing in the fridge overnight, this will allow the flavour to intensify.

The next day, strain off the rhubarb from the poaching liquid (reserving the rhubarb) and measure it – you need around 300ml liquid for this recipe. It's important to note here that the liquid must taste good! Add the lime juice and, if needed, add more sugar or lime juice for acidity (if you're adding more sugar, add it and then warm through to dissolve).

Gently warm the rhubarb poaching liquid and soak the gelatine leaves in ice-cold water in a small bowl. Remove the liquid from the heat, squeeze out the excess water from the gelatine and stir it into the warm liquid to dissolve. Pour into a heatproof container and allow to cool.

When it has cooled, place in the bowl of a stand mixer and whisk at a medium speed for 15–20 minutes until pale and thick. It will change texture to something frothy – almost meringue-like – and light. Spoon into ramekins or dariole moulds and place in the refrigerator to chill for a minimum of 4 hours.

For the white chocolate sauce, melt the white chocolate either gently over a bain-marie or in the microwave in very short bursts, then stir in the double cream and the vanilla seeds.

Serve the rhubarb moonshine with fresh lychees, the poached rhubarb and the cooled white chocolate sauce.

Lemon Bars with Blood Orange and Lemon Caramel

When I first started working as a chef, I had an aspiration to work at Le Manoir aux Quat' Saisons, perhaps one of the pinnacles of fine French cuisine, dessert and patisserie in the country. I grew up watching Raymond Blanc on TV, and really adored the way he worked and spoke about food. I applied and managed to get a week's worth of work experience locked in. I stayed with a lovely lady called Mrs Mott and the whole week felt like a dream. Mrs Mott's cottage was like something out of a film, it was so classically British in its décor. Frills, wallpaper, doilies, the lot. Mrs Mott was such a wonderful host and always made sure that I ate breakfast every morning before I went off to work.

The grounds of Le Manoir were something else: extensive gardens, flowers, vegetable patches, the works. The kitchens too were immaculate and vast. It was – and remains – a big operation. I spent the week in pastry and got a glimpse of how the pros do it. A room for bread and lamination, a section for chocolate work and a **WHOLE ROOM** dedicated to storing the hand-made truffles, as well as a section for ice cream and one for service. The team were very generous with their knowledge and talked me through all their techniques and efforts. I was lucky enough to sample nearly everything in that kitchen, and the small details that went into each element made a huge difference. This dish is an ode to that time.

Lemon Bars with Blood Orange and Lemon Caramel

Makes 6

For the lemon bars
1 'platinum grade' gelatine leaf
    (I use Dr. Oetker)
300g double cream
90g caster sugar
juice of 2 unwaxed lemons

For the cocoa butter dip
100g cocoa butter
20g white chocolate, chopped

For the white chocolate cloud
10g white chocolate
15g/1 tbsp tapioca maltodextrin

For the candied lemon zest
zest of 2 unwaxed lemons (from
    the lemon bars)
30ml water
30g caster sugar

For the lemon caramel
100g caster sugar
20g unsalted butter
140g double cream
20ml lemon juice

To garnish
basil leaves
blood orange pieces
chopped smoked almonds

To make the lemon bars, soak the gelatine in ice-cold water in a small bowl.

Remove the zest from the lemons in strips and set aside for the candied lemon zest.

Heat the cream and sugar in a saucepan until it just starts to boil, then remove from the heat and add the lemon juice. Squeeze out the excess water from the gelatine and stir it into the warmed cream mixture.

Put a silicone tray with six bar moulds on a flat surface, evenly divide the lemon cream mixture between the moulds and level off with an offset spatula. Freeze overnight.

For the cocoa butter shell, warm the cocoa butter until melted, then stir in the white chocolate until melted. Pour into a container deep enough to fit one of the lemon bars in.

Remove the lemon bars from their moulds and quickly dip each into the cocoa butter mixture. The mixture should be runny, but not hot. If it is too hot it will melt the bar but it needs to be just runny enough to evenly coat the bars. After dipping, place on a tray lined with baking paper. Place in the fridge to chill; this will defrost the lemon filling while keeping it encased in the cocoa butter shell.

You will have some cocoa butter shell leftover, it will keep in an airtight container for a week, simply re-warm to use again.

For the white chocolate cloud, melt the white chocolate (see page 41) and stir in the tapioca maltodextrin. Set aside in an airtight container.

For the candied lemon zest, finely julienne the zest you removed from the lemon earlier, removing the pith. Blanch in boiling water for a few seconds three times over, refreshing the water each time.

Gently melt the sugar and measured water together in a saucepan to make a syrup. Add the lemon zest and warm through for 10 minutes. Pour into a heatproof container and cover.

Finally, make the lemon caramel. Put the sugar into a saucepan and warm gently until it turns into a light caramel. Whisk in the butter until smooth over a low heat. Add the cream and lemon juice and leave over a low heat until it just starts to bubble. Take off the heat and allow to cool before using.

Demould and gently place the lemon bars on six serving plates. Dress the plates with the lemon caramel and spoon the white chocolate cloud over the tops of the lemon bars.

Delicately place the candied lemon zest on the plates with the basil leaves, blood orange pieces and chopped smoked almonds.

Serve chilled.

Index

A

almonds: almond jaconde sponge 144–6
  brown butter and chocolate chip financiers 30
  'granola' 158
  oaty Terri biscuits 44
  quince and smoked almond tart 118–19
apples: apple and rosemary tarte tatin 126–7
  fruit pies 106–8
  mincemeat 131
  peach, raspberry and apple cobbler 125
  toffee apple self-saucing pudding 28
apricot jam: chocolate and apricot glaze 155
autumn spiced syrup 147

B

baked NY cheesecake 60–1
bananas: banana fritters 105
  passion cake 32–5
Basque cheesecake 63
batter-style waffles 87
bay leaves: coconut and bay whipped panna cotta 152
berries: red berry compote 149
  soufflé pancakes with berries 194
  see also blueberries; raspberries etc
biscuits 36–51
  crunchy chocolate sandwich biscuits 50
  Dutch shortcake biscuits 49
  gingernuts with white chocolate cream 45
  Indian semolina shortbread (nankhatai) 48
  not-what-you-think chocolate cookies 41
  oaty Terri biscuits 44
  orange, pecan and milk chocolate cookies 46
  Rav in Maryland 40
  roasted hazelnut, blueberry and

mascarpone cookies 47
blueberries: roasted hazelnut, blueberry and mascarpone cookies 47
bombolini, ricotta 104
bran flakes: bran flake and milk chocolate ice cream 177
  'granola' 158
  miso caramel and chocolate tart 133–4
brandy: mincemeat 131
bread: sourdough crumbs 158
brioche dough: the brioche cube 74–7
  fried pillows 103
brown butter and chocolate chip financiers 30
brunsviger with cardamom, pecan and sesame 91
buns: cheese and jam buns 84–6
  Devonshire splits 79
  prune and chocolate buns 80
buttercream: coffee buttercream 152
  whole egg buttercream 16
buttermilk: brunsviger 91
  LPC (lazy person's cake) 24–7

C

cacao nib tuiles 157
cakes 10–35
  brown butter and chocolate chip financiers 30
  cherry and ricotta cake 31
  crème fraîche loaf 23
  LPC (lazy person's cake) 24–7
  mistake cake 15–17
  olive oil, semolina, cardamom and rose cake 35
  passion cake 32–5
  ras malai cake 20–1
  see also sheet sponges
candied lemon zest 200
caramel: apple and rosemary tarte tatin 126–7
  the brioche cube 74–7
  caramelized chocolate mousse 153

caramelized white chocolate ganache 148
  chocolate, caramel tart of dreams 171
  crème brûlée custard 151
  hazelnut praline paste 150
  lemon caramel 199–201
  miso caramel and chocolate tart 133–4
  miso caramel ice cream 176
  popcorn and rosemary caramel 157
  quick toffee sauce 105
  raspberry caramel 148
  toffee apple self-saucing pudding 28
cardamom pods: brunsviger 91
  gulab jamum 100–1
  olive oil, semolina, cardamom and rose cake 35
  ras malai cake 20–1
carrots: passion cake 32–5
cheese: cheese and jam buns 84–6
  kadaif pie 135–6
  roasted Delica pumpkin, feta and rye galette 122–3
  spicy potato, chilli and cheese choux 109
  see also cream cheese; ricotta
cheesecakes 52–69
  baked NY cheesecake 60–1
  Basque cheesecake 63
  Japanese cheesecake 56–8
  mango cheesecake tart 64–5
  no-bake white chocolate cheesecake 59
  rhubarb and orange cheesecake 66–9
cherries: cherry and ricotta cake 31
  cherry lemon pie 114–16
chillies: roasted Delica pumpkin, feta and rye galette 122–3
  spicy potato, chilli and cheese choux 109
chocolate: bran flake and milk chocolate ice cream 177
  brown butter and chocolate chip financiers 30

cacao nib tuiles 157

caramelized chocolate mousse 153

caramelized white chocolate ganache 148

chocolate and apricot glaze 155

chocolate, caramel tart of dreams 171

chocolate magic shell 154

chocolate, peanut and damson tart 117

chocolate sauce 191–2

cocoa butter dip 200

crunchy chocolate sandwich biscuits 50

crystallized white chocolate 159

dark chocolate ganache 133–4

Dutch shortcake biscuits dipped in chocolate 49

gingernuts with white chocolate cream 45

light flourless chocolate cake 145

LPC (lazy person's cake) 24–7

malt chocolate ganache 24–7

miso caramel and chocolate tart 133–4

no-bake white chocolate cheesecake 59

not-what-you-think chocolate cookies 41

oaty Terri biscuits 44

orange, pecan and milk chocolate cookies 46

peanut butter and raspberry ice cream with chocolate 180

prune and chocolate buns 80

Rav in Maryland 40

salted dark chocolate ganache 150

short chocolate and peanut pastry 117, 146

white chocolate sauce 195–6

yogurt glaze 154

choux pastry: spicy potato, chilli and cheese choux 109

cobbler: peach, raspberry and apple cobbler 125

cocoa butter dip 200

coconut: coconut meringue strips 157

coconut cream: coconut and bay whipped panna cotta 152

coconut and lime ice cream 181

coffee: coffee buttercream 152

espresso syrup 147

condensed milk: ras malai cake 20–1

cookies see biscuits

coriander: dipping sauce 109

crabapple jelly: cheese and jam buns 84–6

cranberries: mincemeat 131

cream: caramelized white chocolate ganache 148

chocolate and apricot glaze 155

crème brûlée custard 151

custard 76–7

dark chocolate ganache 133–4

Devonshire splits 79

lemon bars 199–201

malt chocolate ganache 24–7

passion fruit and Greek yogurt mousse 153

pistachio cream 23

pistachio custard 189

quick toffee sauce 105

salted dark chocolate ganache 150

white chocolate sauce 195–6

see also coconut cream; ice cream

cream cheese: cream cheese icing 34

cream cheese pastry 131

kadaif pie 135–6

white chocolate cream 45

see also cheesecakes

crème brûlée custard 151

crème fraîche: baked NY cheesecake 60–1

batter-style waffles 87

crème fraîche loaf 23

crème pâtissière, hazelnut 191–2

crisps, fruit 159

crumble, spiced 156

crunchy bits, entremets 142, 156–9

crystallized white chocolate 159

currants: mincemeat 131

custard: the brioche cube 74–7

crème brûlée custard 151

pistachio custard 189

D

dacquoise, crunchy hazelnut 146

damsons: chocolate, peanut and damson tart 117

deep-frying 92–109

banana fritters 105

fried pillows 103

fruit pies 106–8

gulab jamum 100–1

ricotta bombolini 104

simple sugar ring doughnuts 96–7

spicy potato, chilli and cheese choux 109

Devonshire splits 79

dip, cocoa butter 200

dipping sauce 109

doughnuts, simple sugar ring 96–7

dumplings: gulab jamum 100–1

Dutch shortcake biscuits 49

E

elderflower: lemon and elderflower syrup 147

entremets 138–71

chocolate, caramel tart of dreams 171

crunchy bits 142, 156–9

glazes or garnishes 142, 154–5

mousses or fillers 142, 151–3

OTT opera cake 164–6

sheet sponges 142, 144–6

soaking syrups 142, 147

spreadables 142, 148–50

tropical roulade 168–9

espresso syrup 147

F

financiers, brown butter and chocolate chip 30

flourless chocolate cake 145

focaccia, roasted grape (schiacciata all'uva) 82–3

frangipane, smoked almond 118–19

fried pillows 103
fritters, banana 105
fruit: fruit crisps 159
  fruit jelly 155
  fruit pies 106–8

G
galette: roasted Delica pumpkin, feta and rye galette 122–3
ganache: caramelized white chocolate ganache 148
  dark chocolate ganache 133–4
  malt chocolate ganache 24–7
  salted dark chocolate ganache 150
garlic: roasted Delica pumpkin, feta and rye galette 122–3
gingernuts with white chocolate cream 45
glazes: chocolate and apricot glaze 155
  entremets 142, 154–5
  yogurt glaze 154
'granola' 158
grapes: roasted grape focaccia (schiacciata all'uva) 82–3
gulab jamum 100–1

H
hazelnuts: crunchy hazelnut dacquoise 146
  hazelnut crème pâtissière 191–2
  hazelnut praline paste 150
  miso caramel and chocolate tart 133–4
  prune and chocolate buns 80
  roasted hazelnut, blueberry and mascarpone cookies 47
  roasted hazelnut soufflé 191–2

I
ice cream 172–83
  bran flake and milk chocolate ice cream 177
  coconut and lime ice cream 181
  mango ice cream 182
  miso caramel ice cream 176
  peanut butter and raspberry ice cream 180
icing: cream cheese icing 34
  see also ganache

Indian semolina shortbread (nankhatai) 48

J
jaconde sponge 144–6
jam: cheese and jam buns 84–6
  chocolate and apricot glaze 155
  peanut butter and raspberry ice cream 180
Japanese cheesecake 56–8
jelly, fruit 155

K
kadaif pie 135–6

L
lemon: candied lemon zest 200
  cherry lemon pie 114–16
  lemon and elderflower syrup 147
  lemon bars 199–201
  lemon caramel 199–201
  mincemeat 131
Liège waffles 88
lime: coconut and lime ice cream 181
  lime curd 149
LPC (lazy person's cake) 24–7
lychees, rhubarb moonshine with 195–6

M
magic shell, chocolate 154
malt: malt chocolate ganache 24–7
  roasted peanut and malt sponge 145
mangoes: mango cheesecake tart 64–5
  mango ice cream 182
mascarpone: roasted hazelnut, blueberry and mascarpone cookies 47
meringue: coconut meringue strips 157
  crunchy hazelnut dacquoise 146
  torched meringue 155
milk: custard 76–7
  see also ice cream
mince pies 130–1
miso: miso caramel and chocolate tart 133–4
  miso caramel ice cream 176

mistake cake 15–17
mousses 142, 151–3
  caramelized chocolate mousse 153
  passion fruit and Greek yogurt mousse 153
mozzarella: kadaif pie 135–6

N
nankhatai (Indian semolina shortbread) 48
no-bake white chocolate cheesecake 59
not-what-you-think chocolate cookies 41
NY cheesecake 60–1

O
oats: 'granola' 158
  oaty Terri biscuits 44
olive oil: LPC (lazy person's cake) 24–7
  olive oil, semolina, cardamom and rose cake 35
opera cake 164–6
oranges: crème fraîche loaf 23
  lemon bars with blood orange 199–201
  mincemeat 131
  orange, pecan and milk chocolate cookies 46
  rhubarb and orange cheesecake 66–9
OTT opera cake 164–6

P
pancakes, soufflé 194
panna cotta 152
passion cake 32–5
passion fruit: cream cheese icing 34
  passion fruit and Greek yogurt mousse 153
pastry 106, 114, 142
  choux pastry 109
  cream cheese pastry 131
  rough puff pastry 123
  short chocolate and peanut pastry 117, 146
  sweet pastry 118–19
peach, raspberry and apple cobbler 125

peanut butter: chocolate, peanut and damson tart 117
  peanut butter and raspberry ice cream 180
peanuts: roasted peanut and malt sponge 145
  short chocolate and peanut pastry 117, 146
  sweet and salty peanuts 156
pecan nuts: brunsviger 91
  orange, pecan and milk chocolate cookies 46
pies 110–13
  fruit pies 106–8
  kadaif pie 135–6
  mince pies 130–1
  see also tarts
pillows, fried 103
pistachio praline paste: pistachio cream 23
  pistachio custard 189
pistachios: kadaif pie 135–6
plums, roasted 23
popcorn and rosemary caramel 157
potatoes: spicy potato, chilli and cheese choux 109
praline paste, hazelnut 150
prune and chocolate buns 80
pumpkin: roasted Delica pumpkin, feta and rye galette 122–3
pumpkin seeds: 'granola' 158

Q
quince and smoked almond tart 118–19

R
raisins: mincemeat 131
ras malai cake 20–1
raspberries: no-bake white chocolate cheesecake with raspberries 59
  peach, raspberry and apple cobbler 125
  peanut butter and raspberry ice cream 180
  raspberry caramel 148
  raspberry soufflé 189–90
Rav in Maryland 40
red berry compote 149
rhubarb: rhubarb and orange

cheesecake 66–9
  rhubarb moonshine 195–6
ricotta: cherry and ricotta cake 31
  ricotta bombolini 104
rose extract: olive oil, semolina, cardamom and rose cake 35
rosemary: apple and rosemary tarte tatin 126–7
  popcorn and rosemary caramel 157
rough puff pastry 123
roulade, tropical 168–9
rum syrup 147

S
saffron: gulab jamum 100–1
  ras malai cake 20–1
salted dark chocolate ganache 150
sauces: chocolate sauce 191–2
  dipping sauce 109
  pistachio custard 189
  quick toffee sauce 105
  white chocolate sauce 195–6
schiacciata all'uva (roasted grape focaccia) 82–3
semolina: Indian semolina shortbread (nankhatai) 48
  olive oil, semolina, cardamom and rose cake 35
sesame seeds: brunsviger 91
  'granola' 158
sheet sponges 142, 144–6
  almond jaconde sponge 144–6
  light flourless chocolate cake 145
  roasted peanut and malt sponge 145
  short chocolate and peanut pastry 146
shortbread: Dutch shortcake biscuits 49
  Indian semolina shortbread (nankhatai) 48
smoked almond frangipane 118–19
soaking syrups 142, 147
soufflés 189
  raspberry soufflé 189–90
  roasted hazelnut soufflé 191–2
soufflé pancakes with berries 194
sourdough crumbs 158
soured cream: Basque cheesecake 63

mango cheesecake tart 64–5
spiced crumble 156
sponge see sheet sponges
spreadables, entremets 142, 148–50
sugar syrup 80
sultanas: mincemeat 131
sweet and salty peanuts 156
sweet doughs 70–91
sweet pastry 118–19
syrups, soaking 142, 147
  autumn spiced syrup 147
  espresso syrup 147
  lemon and elderflower syrup 147
  rum syrup 147
  sugar syrup 80

T
tarts 110–13
  apple and rosemary tarte tatin 126–7
  cherry lemon pie 114–16
  chocolate, caramel tart of dreams 171
  chocolate, peanut and damson tart 117
  mango cheesecake tart 64–5
  miso caramel and chocolate tart 133–4
  quince and smoked almond tart 118–19
  roasted Delica pumpkin, feta and rye galette 122–3
  see also pies
Terri biscuits 44
toffee: quick toffee sauce 105
  toffee apple self-saucing pudding 28
torched meringue 155
tropical roulade 168–9
tuiles, cacao nib 157

W
waffles: batter-style waffles 87
  Liège waffles 88
walnuts: passion cake 32–5
whole egg buttercream 16

Y
yogurt: passion fruit and Greek yogurt mousse 153
  yogurt glaze 154

Thank You

A thank you to you, dear reader, fellow sugar lover. Without the support from the first book this one wouldn't have been possible so – thank you.

A massive shout out to the Pavilion team for believing in my ideas from the get-go. Helen Lewis for the lengthy chats that helped to shape my ideas, Cara Armstrong for working so closely with me and being on hand for anything and everything, from personal reassurance, manic questions and even a step-in hand model for the Ras Malai Cake – thanks Cara!

Laura Russell for her vision and work on the aesthetic of this book, Laura loves sweet things and that makes me very happy.

Komal Patel, Lucy Bannell and Alice Sambrook too.

The fabulous shoot team including Ellis Parrinder who made the whole experience very easy and just 'got it.' Stand out food stylist Valerie Berry who has a vivid and incredible imagination, I quickly learnt to not question any of her decisions because they were always correct!

Prop stylist Alexander Breeze, who not only has a soothing voice but a really amazing eye for detail. The book wouldn't look as gorgeous without this lot!

My agent Ben Clark who's one of the good ones! I also have to continuously throw gratitude Steph Milner's way, she is always there as an ear and guide even though she doesn't have to be. I also want to thank Godwin Associates for sticking with me through the first book.

I was lucky to have some great honest recipe testers who helped to make the recipes reliable. A big thank you to Cherlisa Engutsamy, Bhavin Ragha, Tom Kimche, Livia Rett, Sam Tucker, Mattie Taiano, Sam Wong, Josep Gay-Costa, Rahul and Neel Bose and Rosie Fletcher.

Terri Mercieca for the real feedback and help with taking some of my ideas to the next level, Terri, Ruth Tienan Whittle and the Happy Endings team made me feel very welcome in their kitchen when I was testing this book.

More thank yous to Liam Charles for being a good sport and a laugh, Natalie Dormer, Sarah Kern, Alvin Engutsamy and Harriet Gower my support team!

Max Coltart, Kitty Slydell-Cooper and Aman Ramkumar for helping to get Countertalk back off the ground brilliantly.

Jay Patel, my neighbour, who ate his way through my various tests and would come to the fence every time I called him.

My parents and brother for building my resilience, whether they know it or not, and supporting me through the writing of this book. Biji my bestie, who served as my kitchen porter throughout the tests.

The *OFM* team for their continuous support and the *Guardian Feast* team.

To the *Telegraph* for the column opportunity and to the *Telegraph* food team for supporting me.

Everyone who has supported and helped me – you know who you are!

And finally, a big look up to the sky **THANK YOU UNIVERSE** and thank you life.

About the Author

Author of the bestselling *A Pastry Chef's Guide*, Ravneet Gill studied at Le Cordon Bleu before taking over the pastry sections at St. John, Llewelyn's and Wild by Tart. Now a freelance chef, she set up industry networking forum Countertalk in 2018 and in 2020 she was announced as the new technical judge on Channel 4's *Junior Bake Off*, starring alongside Liam Charles. She is the *Telegraph*'s Pastry specialist, as well as a regular columnist for *Guardian Feast*.

First published in the UK in 2021 by
Pavilion Books Company Limited
43 Great Ormond Street
London
WC1N 3HZ

ISBN: 9781911663829

A CIP catalogue record for this book is available from the British Library.

Reproduction by Rival Colour Ltd., UK
Printed and bound by 1010 International Ltd., China

10 9 8 7 6 5 4 3 2 1

www.pavilionbooks.com

Publisher: Helen Lewis
Commissioning editor: Cara Armstrong
Design manager: Laura Russell
Layout designer: Hannah Naughton
Photographer Ellis Parrinder
Prop stylist: Alexander Breeze
Food stylist: Valerie Berry
Makeup artist: Gerri Kitenge
Copyeditor: Lucy Bannell
Production controller: Phil Brown
Illustrations: Tobatron

MIX
Paper from
responsible sources
FSC® C016973
www.fsc.org